Map of the
South Eastern and Chatham Railway

EXCLUDING SUBURBAN AREA

D0811582

nstow
harnal St
Beluncle
Middle Stoke
Grain
Port Victoria
Dockyard
SHEERNESS ON SEA
Sheerness (East)
E. Minster-on-Sea
Minster
Eastchurch
Harty Rd
Leysdown
(Pier)
QUEENBOROUGH
Brambledown
Sheppey
Swale Halt
Rainham
ton
SITTINGBOURNE
Teynham
FAVERSHAM
WHITSTABLE Harbour
Town
HERNE BAY
Blean & Tyler Hill Halt
Grove Ferry
Sturry
Birchington-on-Sea
Westgate
(West)
MARGATE (Sands)
Broadstairs
RAMSGATE (Harbour)
(Town)
Minster
Sandwich

(East)
rsted & Thurnham
Hollingbourne
Harrietsham
Lenham
Charing
Selling
(West)
CANTERBURY (East)
Chartham
South Bridge
Chilham
Bishopsbourne
Barham
Bekesbourne
Adisham
E K R
Shepherds Well
DEAL
Walmer
Headcorn
Pluckley
Hothfield
Wye
Elham
Kearsney
Martin Mill
K & E S R
ASHFORD
Smeeth
Lyminge
Shorncliffe Central
(Priory)
DOVER (Harbour)
Pier
Town
(Junction)
Ham St & Orleston
Westenhanger
Sandling Jn
HYTHE
Sandgate
FOLKESTONE HARBOUR
CALAIS
Appledore
Tenterden
Brookland
New Romney & Littlestone
Lydd
RYE
inchelsea
Dungeness
BOULOGNE
GS

| Scale (Approx) | 0 | 5 | 10 | 15 | 20 | Miles |

SECR LBSC JOINT ▬▬▬▬▬▬▬

South Eastern & Chatham Railway Album

South Eastern & Chatham Railway Album

P.K.Jones

LONDON
IAN ALLAN LTD

Contents

The photographs reproduced in this book represent a fraction of the material held by the Real Photographs Co whose combined collection spans the whole of British railway history. Order forms for these photographs and lists of the rest of the collection can be obtained by sending an SAE to:

Real Photographs Co
Terminal House
Shepperton
TW17 8AS

Cover: SECR 'E' Class 4-4-0 No 516 on a passenger working c1921. *LGRP 28514*
The LGRP photographs are reproduced by courtesy of David & Charles

First published 1984

ISBN 0 7110 1345 4

Published by Ian Allan Ltd, Shepperton, Surrey; and printed by Ian Allan Printing Ltd at their works at Coombelands in Runnymede, England.

The South Eastern Railway

The South Eastern Railway was sanctioned by Parliament on 21 June 1836, originally for a line to run from the London & Croydon Railway's terminus at London Bridge and thence over the London & Greenwich Railway to Corbett's Lane whence it was to run to Folkestone and Dover. In order to serve as many towns as possible, the route zig-zagged somewhat after Oxted so that it passed through Tonbridge, Maidstone and Ashford. The following year authority was obtained to link up with the London and Croydon Railway at Norwood and use that company's tracks to Corbett's Lane. Also in 1837 the London & Brighton Railway was authorised from Norwood to Brighton and, since this line was to run parallel to the South Eastern's for some distance south of Norwood, it was suggested by Parliament that costs could be considerably reduced if the two companies were to share tracks over this distance. As a result, this section of the line, between Norwood and Redhill, was built jointly and was opened on 12 July 1841, the South Eastern having running powers only until 19 July 1842 when it purchased the southern portion from Coulsdon to Redhill. At Redhill the line turned eastwards and then ran in an almost straight line to Ashford and on to Folkestone and Dover. The first section of the South Eastern proper, from Redhill to Tonbridge, was opened on 26 May 1842 and on 7 February 1844 Dover was reached with the opening of the final section from Folkestone.

The engineer of the line was William Cubitt who used track with transverse wooden sleepers instead of the usual stone blocks. The construction was fairly straightforward until Folkestone was reached, fast running being provided for by easy gradients and building the stations at Tonbridge, Paddock Wood and Ashford with through lines.

At Folkestone it was necessary to build a viaduct across the Foord gap and a temporary station was provided until the new station was opened on 18 December 1843. The engineering work between Folkestone and Dover was considerable, four tunnels — the Martello, Abbot's Cliff, Shakespeare and Archcliffe — being cut through solid chalk and between Abbot's Cliff and Shakespeare tunnels the Round Down cliff was blown up to make way for the new line.

When the South Eastern started to run its trains into London Bridge on 26 May 1842 it was the fourth company after the London & Greenwich, London & Croydon and London & Brighton to do so. The original station had been built by the London & Greenwich and opened in 1836 and in 1839 the London & Croydon opened its own station adjacent to and to the north of the original station. By then the South Eastern and the London & Brighton had been sanctioned to run into London Bridge so authority was obtained to lay two more tracks between the terminus and Corbett's Lane where the lines diverged. These two additional tracks (which were laid in 1842) were to the south of the original two and were for the use of the London & Croydon, London & Brighton and South Eastern railways. This meant that the trains of these three companies would have to cross the path of the London & Greenwich in order to enter their platforms at London Bridge and, as a result, it was agreed that ownership of the two parts of the station should be exchanged, this taking place in 1844.

At first the London & Greenwich charged a toll of 3d per passenger for the use of its line but after the widening of 1842 was carried out this was increased to $4\frac{1}{2}$d. This caused considerable resentment and in 1843 the South Eastern and London & Croydon railways obtained Parliamentary sanction for a branch line just south of Corbett's Lane to a new terminus station known as Bricklayer's Arms thereby avoiding the London & Greenwich's line and its toll. Opening took place on 1 May 1844 and all the London & Croydon's and half the South Eastern's trains were routed into the new terminus. The resultant loss of revenue brought the London & Greenwich to the negotiating table and an agreement was reached whereby the South Eastern was to lease the London & Greenwich's line for a period of 999 years, this taking effect from 1 January 1845. The Bricklayer's Arms terminus was not popular with passengers and, having served its purpose, all regular passenger services were withdrawn in 1846 but it remained in use as an important goods station. London Bridge therefore resumed its importance and in 1847 the South Eastern obtained Parliamentary sanction to enlarge the station and lay two more tracks as far as Corbett's Lane.

Meanwhile there had been developments in other areas which resulted in a branch line being opened from Paddock Wood to Maidstone on 25 September 1844 and a line from Ashford to Canterbury on 6 February 1846. Later the same year extensions were opened from Canterbury to Ramsgate and thence to Margate Sands and on 1 July 1847 a branch from Minster on this line was opened to Deal.

The Thames & Medway Canal was purchased in 1846 and this provided an almost ready-made route to north Kent. The canal had been opened in 1824 from the Thames at Gravesend to a point on the Medway opposite Rochester and in 1845 a single track railway laid along the towpath had been opened. This canal had taken 24 years to complete and involved much difficult constructional work, chiefly the cutting of two tunnels through $2\frac{1}{4}$ miles of chalk, with only 50yds between the end of one tunnel and the start of the next. The canal was drained and a double track line laid and opened between Gravesend and Strood on 23 August 1847. The line was extended westward from Gravesend to North Kent East Junction near London Bridge and on 30 July 1849 the through route between London Bridge and Strood was opened.

An independent company, the Reading, Guildford & Reigate Railway, was promoted locally to link the GWR at Reading with the South Eastern at Redhill. It was opened in sections during 1849 making use of running powers over the LSWR between Shalford Junction and Ash Junction. Because it formed a useful link between the Great Western and the Channel ports and resorts it was supported and leased by the South Eastern from its inception and purchased in 1852.

The Brighton, Lewes & Hastings company was empowered in 1845 to extend its Brighton to Lewes line, then under construction, from Lewes to Hastings and Ashford but Parliament decided that the section from Bopeep Junction (near Hastings) to Ashford could be better operated by the South Eastern and accordingly this section was transferred, opening taking place on 13 February 1851. A branch line from Tonbridge to Tunbridge Wells had been opened on 20 February 1845 and in 1851/52 this was extended to Hastings, thereby producing a shorter route than the one via Ashford.

By this time the South Eastern was actively developing its facilities at Folkestone. The harbour at Dover was government owned and so its efforts were concentrated at Folkestone which had a steamer service to Boulogne, the communications between there and the rest of France being much better than those at Calais, the destination of the Dover steamers. At first the facilities at Folkestone were inadequate and the steamers could only berth at high tide but improvements were made and by the time the new Harbour station was brought into use in 1850 they could berth at most tides. There was a steep gradient of around 1 in 30 leading down to the Harbour station and the low axle load permitted over the swing bridge linking the original railway pier with the station restricted the types of locomotives that could be used. In order to cope with the gradual increase in size of the steamers a new pier which jutted out into the sea was completed in 1863.

In 1853 powers were obtained to extend the line from Maidstone to Strood, the opening taking place on 18 June 1856.

Also in 1853 the South Eastern purchased the Canterbury & Whitstable Railway having worked it since 1844. This company was the first to carry passengers in trains hauled by a steam locomotive having been opened on 3 May 1830.

An independent company, the Charing Cross Railway, was authorised in 1859 to construct a line from London Bridge to a new terminus station on the north bank of the Thames at Charing Cross. In 1861 authority was obtained for an extension into an additional terminus at Cannon Street, also on the north bank of the Thames, the main section into Charing Cross being opened on 11 January 1864 and the extension into Cannon Street on 1 September 1866. Although Cannon Street was well sited for the City the South Eastern's practice of making most trains running from London Bridge to Charing Cross call there created considerable congestion because of the reversal of direction and change of engine involved. A single line connection was made between the new line and the LSWR terminus at Waterloo and on 1 January 1869 a new station known as Waterloo Junction was opened adjacent to the LSWR terminus.

While the South Eastern was developing its port at Folkestone the harbour at Dover was being developed by the Admiralty. In 1847 work was started on the Admiralty Pier which was to facilitate the transfer of goods. Until 1854 the mails were conveyed by Admiralty packets to Dover and thence by the SER overland but in that year a contract for the sea passage was given to the local firm of Jenkins and Churchward. The SER continued to carry the mails from Dover and in 1860 started to run its trains directly on to the

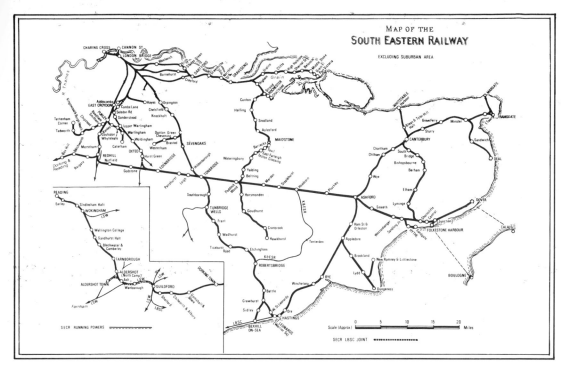

MAP OF THE
SOUTH EASTERN RAILWAY
EXCLUDING SUBURBAN AREA

Admiralty Pier. In 1862 the government decided to place the contract for the carriage of the mails in the hands of a single carrier, and since the SER already had its own steamers, the new contract was offered to them. The South Eastern was concentrating its efforts on Folkestone and possibly underestimated the importance of Dover and the contract was refused. The London Chatham & Dover Railway quickly stepped in and secured the contract and, although the two companies came to an agreement (effective from 20 June 1863) for the joint carriage of the mails over land, the sea passage remained the responsibility of the LCDR. In 1865 the two companies introduced a pooling arrangement for the Continental traffic via Dover and Folkestone whereby the traffic receipts were paid into a joint account and divided on a sliding scale. In 1866 the SER received 68% and the LCDR 32% and by 1872 the receipts were equally divided, a situation which continued thereafter.

The emergence of the LCDR as a serious competitor in the early 1860s prompted the call by some of the South Eastern shareholders for more vigorous leadership and this led to Edward Watkin, the chairman of the Manchester Sheffield and Lincolnshire Railway, joining the board in 1865 and becoming chairman the following year. So began the rivalry between the SER and the LCDR which became a personal feud between Watkin and his opposite number Forbes.

The opening of the LCDR's line to Dover in 1861 meant that the South Eastern would have to compete for the traffic between London and Dover. The route via Redhill then in use was longer than necessary and the section shared with the LBSCR was congested and subject to delays. As a result, a new line from New Cross (St John's) to Tonbridge was proposed, this saving 13 miles on the old route. Parliamentary sanction was obtained in 1862 and it was opened in sections between 1 July 1865 and 1 May 1868.

A branch line from Sandling Junction, on the main line between Ashford and Folkestone, via Hythe to Sandgate was sanctioned in 1864 and opened on 9 October 1874.

The opening in 1876 by the LCDR of the Queenborough Pier Branch to provide a connection with the Steamer service to Flushing was interpreted by the South Eastern as a means of avoiding the 'Continental Agreement' of 1863. The South Eastern therefore supported the independent Hundred of Hoo Railway which obtained powers to build a line from Hoo Junction on the North Kent line to Port Victoria on the Isle of Grain opposite Queenborough. In 1881 this company was taken over by the South Eastern, the line being opened throughout on 11 September 1882. A deep water pier was built and a ferry service to Queenborough introduced but Port Victoria was not a success and the ferry service was withdrawn in 1901 and the pier closed in 1916.

Several independent companies promoted

lines in the South Eastern's territory about this time which resulted in the opening of branch lines to Westerham, Dungeness, New Romney and Hayes and of a new line between Shorncliffe and Canterbury. All these companies were worked and eventually taken over by the SER.

Relations with the LCDR became even more strained in 1886 when a dispute arose over the 'Continental Agreement' of 1865, a dispute which was not resolved until 1890 when the House of Lords ruled against the South Eastern.

In 1894 Sir Edward Watkin resigned as chairman due to ill health and relations with the LCDR consequently improved. Negotiations were started with the LCDR and in 1898 agreement for a working union of the two companies was finally reached whereby each company was to retain its legal and financial identity but for engineering and operating matters they were to be worked as one company.

1
A Charing Cross-Hastings train passing Halstead Knockholt headed by a Westinghouse brake-fitted 'A' class 4-4-0. *LGRP 21970*

2
A Dover boat express passing Chislehurst headed by 'B' class 4-4-0 No 448 soon after being built in 1898. *LGRP 21256*

3
'Q' class 0-4-4T No 73 near Brasted on the Westerham Branch. *LGRP 21979*

4
A down express passing Grove Park about 1900 headed by 'B' class 4-4-0 No 454. *LGRP 21254*

5
'O' class 0-6-0 No 301 seen here passing through Grove Park with a down goods train about 1901. *LGRP 21251*

1

2

6

7

8

6
Another view taken at Grove Park about 1901, this time showing 'B' class 4-4-0 No 440 with a down express of mainly six-wheeled stock. *LGRP 21253*

7
A view of Chislehurst station taken in 1914. It was opened as Chislehurst & Bickley Park on 1 July 1865 when the line to New Cross (St Johns) was opened and renamed Chislehurst on 1 September 1866. *LGRP 8210*

8
Kingswood station in 1914. It was opened on 2 November 1897 when the first section of the branch

to Tattenham Corner was opened as far as Kingswood. Note the terrace on top of the platform awning and the three storey station building. *LGRP 8538*

9
Two 'O' class 0-6-0s with No 52 leading passing through Grove Park in 1903 with a down coal train. *LGRP 21328*

10
A view of Kenley station in 1914. It was opened on 5 August 1856 as part of the Caterham Railway which was opened on that day from Purley to Caterham. At first it was known as Coulsdon but it was renamed Kenley in December 1856. *LGRP 8539*

11

12

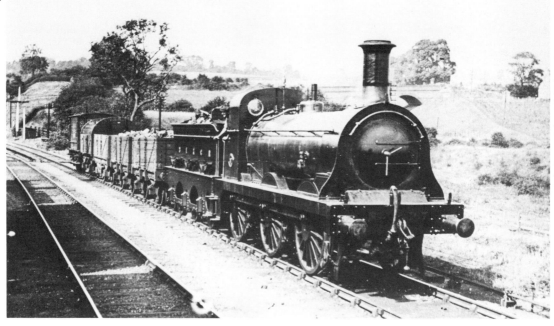

13

11
Caterham, seen here in 1914, was the terminus of the Caterham Railway which was purchased by the South Eastern in 1859. *LGRP 8543*

12
'O' class 0-6-0 No 167 photographed near Merstham, just north of Redhill, with a goods train. *LGRP 15136*

13
'Q1' class 0-4-4T No 366 at Paddock Wood in 1910. This engine was built by Neilson, Reid & Co, in 1891 as a Class Q engine and rebuilt to Class Q1 in April 1906. Withdrawal took place in 1926. *LGRP 17914*

14
'F' class 4-4-0 No 194 seen here with a goods train near Edenbridge. This engine was one of the 12 'Fs' not to be rebuilt as an 'F1', being withdrawn still with its Stirling domeless boiler in 1926. *LGRP 15135*

15
A two-coach train consisting of a bogie tri-composite and a bogie brake third hauled by 'B1' No 455 about 1914. *LGRP 28507*

14

15

16

17

18

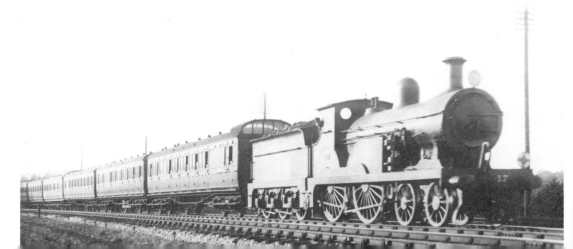

16
A down Hastings express seen here passing Chislehurst in 1914 headed by 'B1' No 452. *LGRP 8208*

17
Ramsgate Town station photographed in 1924. It was opened on 13 April 1846 as Ramsgate and renamed in July 1899 to avoid confusion with the LCDR station. After Grouping a number of improvements were carried out in the area which involved the opening of new lines and the closing of old ones. A new station was opened at Ramsgate and another one at nearby Dumpton Park and the old station at Ramsgate Town was closed on 2 July 1926. *LGRP 8896*

18
A rake of modern SECR bogie stock seen here in about 1920 headed by 'B1' 4-4-0 No 17 which has an extended smokebox. *LGRP 28504*

19
'B1' 4-4-0 No 217 in wartime austerity livery passing Elmstead Woods with the Hastings Pullman. *RP T6019*

20
Canterbury West station in 1924 showing the separate roofs for the up and down platforms and tracks with the uncovered through lines in between. It was opened as Canterbury on 6 February 1846 when the line from Ashford was opened and renamed in July 1899 to avoid confusion with the LCDR station. *LGRP 8894*

21

22

23

21
A train of 12 four- and six-wheelers near Grove Park in September 1921 headed by 'Q' class 0-4-4T No 173; note the Westinghouse brake equipment. *LPC 23149*

22
A view of Knockholt station which was opened as Halstead Knockholt on 1 May 1876 and renamed on 1 October 1900. *LPC 23381*

23
'F1' 4-4-0 No 212 passing Chelsfield with an up train from Sevenoaks. *LGRP 16619*

24
'Q1' class 0-4-4T No 348 in wartime austerity livery passing through Elmstead Woods station with a 14-coach train. *RP T6002*

25
A 1931 view of West St Leonards station. *LGRP 8983*

26
Bopeep Junction and Tunnel viewed from West
St Leonards station in 1931. The section from Bopeep
Junction to Hastings was opened on 13 February 1851
followed on 1 February 1852 by the opening of the
section to Battle in the opposite direction, thereby
completing the line from Tonbridge to Hastings. The
name Bopeep came from that of a local inn.
LGRP 8981

27
Another 1931 view of Bopeep Tunnel, this time viewed
from the St Leonards end. *LGRP 8984*

28
Godstone station was opened on 26 May 1842 when
the Redhill to Tonbridge line was opened. The view
seen here was taken in 1947. *LGRP 12123*

29
A 1932 view of Minster Junction which clearly shows
the staggered platforms. This station was on the
Canterbury to Ramsgate line which was opened on
13 April 1846 and extended southwards from Minster
to Deal on 1 July 1847. *LGRP 11910*

30
Redhill locomotive depot in 1935. It was rebuilt with a
new asbestos roof in 1950 and closed in 1965.
LGRP 8110

31

32

33

31
'B1' 4-4-0 as SR No 1021 photographed at Leysdown
on the Isle of Sheppey in 1936. The articulated motor-
train set No 514 was converted from the carriage units
of two steam railcars. *LGRP 13220*

32
Folkestone Harbour in May 1949 showing an up
Continental express hauled by former SER 'R1' 0-6-0Ts
No 1337 and 1128 and former SECR 'R1' 0-4-4T
No 1708 crossing the swing bridge. *RP K262*

33
Reading locomotive depot photographed in October
1949 and showing 'U1' class 2-6-0 No 31898. It was
closed in 1965. *RP K508*

34
A six-wheeled passenger brake van with look-outs at
both ends at Groombridge in June 1963. *RP K5743*

35
Winchelsea station in 1951 showing the staggered
platforms and signalbox. It was on the Ashford to
Bopeep Junction section which was opened on
13 February 1851. *LGRP 25389*

South Eastern Locomotives

The first engines on the South Eastern were the 12 passenger 2-2-2s ordered from Sharp, Roberts in 1841, the first of which were delivered in December of that year. The South Eastern and the London & Croydon made extensive use of each other's lines and consequently it was decided to pool the locomotives and rolling stock of both companies, a Joint Committee being set up to control this pool. The Joint Committee consisted of three directors each from the two companies plus William Cubitt, the Engineer-in-Chief of the South Eastern, the first meeting taking place on 26 March 1842 when each company had eight locomotives. By the end of that year the remaining four Sharp singles had been delivered and these were joined by five Bury 2-2-0s and one Bury 0-4-0 which brought the Joint Committee's stock up to 26.

The London & Brighton Railway, which also shared running powers with the South Eastern and London & Croydon, had so far kept its locomotives out of the pool but it was eventually decided to join. Accordingly, its 34 locomotives were taken over by the Joint Committee on 1 March 1844 and three of the London & Brighton directors joined the committee. In the meantime, the Joint Committee had purchased 16 more engines, seven 2-2-2s, two 0-6-0s and one 0-4-2 from Sharp's, two 2-2-0s and two 0-4-0s from Bury's and two Rennie 2-2-2s.

However, all was not well: the SER was the dominant partner and made increasing demands on the joint stock to work its new lines. Furthermore, the SER was dissatisfied with the method of calculating the shares of locomotive expenses, which was based on the tonnage of each company's trains, therefore in October 1844 it announced its intention to withdraw from the Joint Committee. In December the other two companies also announced their withdrawal and it was decided that the stock should be divided on 12 April 1845. In anticipation of its withdrawal from the Joint Committee the SER had begun to order engines on its own account and had taken delivery of eight engines in April 1845 which, when added to the Joint Committee's stock of 89, gave a total stock of 97 engines. In addition, a further 26 engines were on order and this total of

36

'Little Mail' 2-2-2 No 147, one of the eight engines built by Sharp Brothers in 1851 and employed principally on the Continental services which led to them being known as the 'Mails'. When they were displaced from these trains by larger singles in the 1860s they were transferred to the Hastings and Ramsgate services and then known as 'Little Mails'. No 147 was rebuilt in 1866 with a boiler having a coal-burning firebox and withdrawn in 1878. *LPC 33055*

123 engines was divided between the three companies, the South Eastern receiving 71, the London & Brighton 44 and the London & Croydon 8. It was also agreed that the Joint Committee should continue to operate until 31 January 1846.

The 71 engines allotted to the SER were of many different types as would be expected at that time and they were, in fact, the products of 11 different manufacturers. Their mainstay was 34 Sharp 5ft 6in 2-2-2s, the more unusual types including a Bodmer 2-2-2 with double-pistoned cylinders and a Borrie 2-2-2 with Chanter's Patent coal-burning firebox. Also included was the celebrated Stephenson long boiler 2-2-2 *White Horse of Kent* which took part in the trials arranged by the Gauge Commissioners in 1845. Despite the unfavourable impression on the commission of this type of locomotive, the SER decided to adopt the long boiler type. James l'Anson Cudworth was appointed Locomotive Superintendent on 22 May 1845 and although there were long boiler engines on order before he took over he persisted with this type for a time, 53 such engines being delivered between 1845 and 1848. He then tried out the Crampton type, converting one Nasmyth and four Bury singles to that type in 1848 and the following year three more were acquired from Tulk & Ley, these being diverted from an order by the Namur & Liège Railway. More unconventional engines appeared in 1851 in the shape of the 10 engines of the 'Folkestone' class. These too were Cramptons but of a later type featuring a dummy crankshaft with outside coupling rods driving the 6ft 0in driving wheels. They were poor performers and had difficulty in starting anything but the lightest trains and consequently all except one were rebuilt to 2-4-0s in 1868/69. While the 'Folkestone' class was being delivered, eight conventional singles were acquired from Sharp's. They proved very successful working the Dover expresses and, as a result, four similar engines were built at the new works at Ashford in 1856/57. Also in 1851 were built five engines of the 'Bulldog' class, these being 0-4-0Ts with a dummy crankshaft placed between the two pairs of wheels. They were used on the Folkestone Harbour branch but suffered from the same fault as the 'Folkestones', lack of adhesion, and in 1859 all were converted to 0-6-0s, three remaining as tank engines but the other two becoming tender engines.

After the break up of the Joint Committee in 1846 the decision was taken to build a new works at the small market town of Ashford. Construction of the first locomotives, 10 long boiler 2-4-0s for the Hastings branch, commenced in 1853, using boilers supplied by Nasmyth's. These engines, known as the 'Hastings' class, proved very successful but four similar ones, built at the same time by Stephenson's, were not a success, their riding and steaming being poor. This was, no doubt, because Cudworth had made a number of changes in their design as compared with those built at Ashford.

Four 0-6-0 tender engines, Nos 171-174, were built at Ashford in 1856, the first of Cudworth's standard goods engines. These first four engines had sandwich frames and boilers with coke-burning fireboxes but, following successful experiments with coal-burning fireboxes, further engines of the class had fireboxes of this type and plate frames instead of the sandwich pattern. Construction continued until 1876 by which time 53 had been built and most of them were rebuilt with domeless boilers during James Stirling's era.

Six double-framed passenger 2-4-0s with 6ft 0in coupled wheels were built by E. B. Wilson in 1857 and were very successful on the Ramsgate stopping trains. They were numbered 179-184, all were rebuilt in 1870/71 with boilers with coal-burning fireboxes and they were withdrawn between 1880 and 1884.

In 1858/59 six double-framed passenger 2-4-0s with 5ft 6in coupled wheels were built at Ashford, use being made of some parts salvaged from scrapped Sharp singles. The use in five engines of secondhand Sharp pattern brass domes led to them being known as 'Little Sharps'.

The success of the Wilson 2-4-0s of 1857 led to the introduction, in 1859, of the generally similar '118' class which had boilers with Cudworth's coal-burning firebox instead of the coke-burning type. This was the largest class of Cudworth engines, a total of 128 being built by 1875 when construction ceased, 86 by Ashford. Many were rebuilt by Stirling with domeless boilers but, although side sheets and weatherboards were provided, the footplate remained open.

In November 1861 two large singles with 7ft 0in driving wheels were turned out of Ashford Works followed in 1862 by four each from Kitson's and the Vulcan Foundry. These 10 engines, which had double frames and Cudworth's coal-burning fireboxes, worked the Continental services, being known as the 'Mails', and in 1865/66 six similar engines were built at Ashford. In 1870 two members of this class took part in a series of trials with two LSWR 2-4-0s, the object being to compare the performance of the Cudworth and Beattie coal-burning fireboxes. By this time it was rather academic since both types had been rendered obsolete by the invention of the simpler brick arch.

During the 1860s three classes of four-coupled well tank engines were introduced which were designed for suburban work in the London area.

The first of these were 12 0-4-2s built in 1863/64 which gave good service for 20 years but which had inadequate fuel and water capacity. As a result a larger version, with a bogie replacing the trailing wheels, was introduced in 1866, seven engines being built by Brassey & Co. The third class of well tanks was the six 0-4-2s built at Ashford in 1867-69 for working goods trains. They were all rebuilt with Stirling boilers between 1880 and 1882 and withdrawn between 1887 and 1893.

As a result of a disagreement between Cudworth and Alfred Watkin, who was in charge of the Operating Department, over what types of locomotive were required, the South Eastern chairman, Sir Edward Watkin, felt it necessary to consult John Ramsbottom the former Locomotive Superintendent of the LNWR who was at that time a consultant. Ramsbottom produced a report which recommended the construction of 20 modern 2-4-0 passenger engines to which the directors agreed. Cudworth was virtually relegated to Ramsbottom's assistant and, not surprisingly, on 14 September 1876 he tendered his resignation. On 11 November Alfred Watkin, the chairman's son, was appointed in his place.

In the meantime the 20 Ramsbottom 2-4-0s had entered service. They were known as the 'Ironclads' and had 6ft 6in coupled wheels, inside frames and Allan straight link motion and somewhat resembled the LNWR 'Precedents'. Unlike the latter, however, they were poor performers and were soon relegated to the Dover and Hastings semi-fasts. They were all rebuilt with Stirling domeless boilers between 1888 and 1891 and they were withdrawn between 1903 and 1906.

Three 0-6-0Ts, Nos 152-154, were built at Ashford in 1877 for working the Folkestone Harbour branch. They were all withdrawn in 1892.

Alfred Watkin did not remain Locomotive Superintendent for long. At the insistence of some of the directors he was prevented by the terms of his employment from engaging in any outside business interests but in the summer of 1877 he was elected a Member of Parliament for Grimsby and consequently he was forced to resign on 6 September. Richard Mansell, who was Locomotive Engineer at Ashford Works, took over temporarily but on 28 March 1878 James Stirling of the Glasgow & South Western Railway was appointed as the new Locomotive Superintendent. While Mansell was in charge, 10 0-6-0 goods tender engines were ordered but only the first three were built, the remaining seven being cancelled by Stirling. Ashford were also in the process of constructing a class of nine 0-4-4 tanks which became known as the 'Gunboats'. They worked suburban trains in the London area

for about 10 years until they were replaced by Stirling's 'Q' class 0-4-4Ts.

Stirling's first South Eastern design appeared in 1878 when the first engines of the 'O' class were completed by Sharp, Stewart. They were 0-6-0 goods tender engines with 5ft 1in wheels, domeless boilers and inside frames, a total of 122 being built, the last in 1899. Commencing in 1903, 59 of them were rebuilt with Wainwright domed boilers and cabs and reclassified 'O1'. Withdrawal started in 1906 and 35 (including one 'O1') had gone by Grouping but 55 (including three which had been sold to the East Kent Railway) survived long enough to be taken over by British Railways and the last survivor, No 31065, lasted until June 1961.

Stirling next produced a class of 12 4-4-0 passenger engines with inside frames and domeless boilers to replace the earlier 2-4-0s then in service. These engines, known as the 'A' class, were rebuilt at Ashford between 1879 and 1881 and were all withdrawn between 1907 and 1909.

In 1880 three 4-4-0Ts were acquired from Beyer, Peacock, these being diverted from an order for the Metropolitan Railway, so that the SER could provide adequate power for working the through trains to the GNR through the Metropolitan's tunnels. The introduction in 1881/82 of 'Q' class condensing tanks soon rendered them redundant and in 1883 all three were sold to the Metropolitan Railway.

Two small tank engines were acquired in 1881 for use in Folkestone Harbour, No 302 being an 0-4-0 crane engine and No 313 and 0-4-0ST. A further crane engine, No 409, was acquired in 1896 for use at Ashford Works where it was joined by No 302 in 1905.

The first engine of a large class of 0-4-4T engines was turned out of Ashford Works in 1881. These engines, known as the 'Q' class, were built for working suburban trains in the London area, a total of 118 being built by 1897 when construction ceased. Between 1903 and 1917 55 of them were rebuilt with Wainwright domed boilers of the same type as was fitted to his 'H' class 0-4-4Ts, the classification being altered to 'Q1'. Withdrawal started in 1906 with the last survivor lasting until 1930.

The growth in passenger traffic plus the introduction of the heavier bogie coaches made it increasingly difficult for the small existing engines to handle the trains. As a result, Stirling introduced the 'F' class 4-4-0s in 1883 to provide more power for the best trains. They had 7ft 0in coupled wheels and Stirling's usual domeless boiler, a total of 88 being built, all at Ashford, between 1883 and 1898. Between 1903 and 1920 76 of them were rebuilt with Wainwright domed boilers and cabs and were reclassified 'F1'. One engine was withdrawn in 1920, this being the only one not to be taken over by the Southern, but only nine were left to enter British Railways stock and these all went by 1949.

The next class to be introduced by Stirling was known as the 'R' class and consisted of 25 0-6-0Ts built at Ashford Works between 1888 and 1898, primarily for use as shunters. Thirteen of them were rebuilt by Wainwright with domed boilers between 1910 and 1922 and these all entered British Railways stock in 1948, the last two surviving until 1960. Of the 12 'Rs', one was withdrawn after an accident in 1914 and the rest all went between 1931 and 1943.

A works shunter for use at Ashford Works was acquired from Manning, Wardle in 1890. It was an 0-6-0ST, No 353, and it lasted until 1929.

An enlarged version of the 'F' class 4-4-0s was introduced in 1898, the principal difference being the boiler which was of 3in greater diameter. These engines were known as the 'B' class and 20, Nos 440-459, were built by Neilson, Reid in 1898. It was intended to build a further 20 at Ashford but in the event only nine were completed, the last 11 being cancelled when Wainwright took over. In service they were little improvement on the 'Fs' and 27 of them were rebuilt with Wainwright domed boilers between 1910 and 1927 and reclassified 'B1', then becoming virtually identical to the 'F1s'. The two remaining 'Fs' were withdrawn in 1930 and 1931 and in 1933 withdrawal of the 'F1s' commenced but 16 were still in service at Nationalisation and the last one survived until 1951.

When, in 1898, the LCDR and the SER decided to form a working union it was also decided that each company's Locomotive Superintendent should be retired and one man appointed in their place. Accordingly, on 27 September 1898 Harry S. Wainwright, the South Eastern's Carriage & Wagon Superintendent, was appointed to the new post of Locomotive, Carriage and Wagon Superintendent and on 31 December James Stirling retired.

37

One of Cudworth's standard goods engines, No 109, which was built at Ashford in 1864. It is shown with the original Cudworth coal-burning firebox but it was later rebuilt with a Stirling domeless boiler. *LPC 33102*

38

39

38

'Little Sharp' 2-4-0 No 19 which was built at Ashford in 1858 incorporating some material from scrapped Sharp singles. The four-wheeled tender had previously run behind the old London & Greenwich 2-2-2 No 7. *LGRP 4168*

39

'Mail' 2-2-2 No 201 which was built by Kitson & Co in 1862 and employed on the Continental expresses. The engines of this class not only took the place of the 1851 Sharp singles on these trains but also took their name of 'Mails' as well. Note the sandbox mounted on the top of the boiler and the Cudworth coal-burning firebox. *LPC 15483*

40

0-4-2WT No 209, one of a batch of 10 built by Slaughter, Gruning & Co in 1864. No 209 was withdrawn in 1886. *LPC 15601*

40

41
One of seven 0-4-4WTs built by Brassey & Co in 1866
for working suburban trains in the London area. This
engine, No 236, was rebuilt in 1880 with a Stirling
domeless boiler and withdrawn in 1889. *LGRP 4165*

42
Six more 'Mails' were built at Ashford in 1865/66, one
of which was No 81, seen here with stovepipe chimney
and Cudworth coal-burning firebox. *LPC 15602*

43
In 1877 three 0-6-0Ts were built at Ashford for
working the Folkestone Branch, No 152 being
illustrated here. All three were withdrawn in 1892
when their duties were taken over by three 'Rs'.
LPC 33370

42

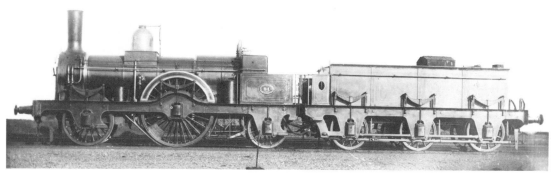

43

44
'Gunboat' 0-4-4T No 58 which was one of a class of nine engines built at Ashford in 1878 during Richard Mansell's brief régime. They worked suburban trains in the London area until they were displaced from these duties by the 'Qs'. No 58 was withdrawn in 1891. *LPC 15600*

45
'O' class 0-6-0 No 315, one of Stirling's standard goods locomotives, 122 of which were built between 1878 and 1899. No 315 was built at Ashford in 1882 and was one of the first of the class to be withdrawn, in 1908. *LGRP 16088*

46
'A' class 4-4-0 No 159 which was built at Ashford in 1880 and withdrawn in 1909. This engine was one of five of the class which between 1901 and 1908 were rebuilt with Wainwright domeless boilers. *LPC 15487*

47
Another view of an 'A' class 4-4-0, this one being No 160 which was also built at Ashford in 1880 but was withdrawn in 1907. *LGRP 17952*

48
0-4-2WT No 73 which was built at Ashford in 1867, the first of a class of six engines built for goods work in the London area. In 1881 it was rebuilt with a Stirling domeless boiler, as shown here, and withdrawn in 1891. *LPC 15489*

45

46

47

48

49

50

51

49
'Q' class 0-4-4T No 27, one of the first batch built at Ashford in 1881/82 with short wheelbase bogie and small bogie wheels. It was withdrawn in 1910. *LGRP 21660*

50
'F' class 4-4-0 No 137 which was built at Ashford in 1891 and rebuilt to Class F1 in 1906. *LPC 15466*

51
'Ironclad' 2-4-0 No 278 which was built by the Avonside Engine Company in 1876 to the requirements of John Ramsbottom and seen here after rebuilding by Stirling in 1889 with a domeless boiler. It was withdrawn in 1906. *LGRP 18251*

52
Cudworth goods 0-6-0 No 44 after rebuilding by Stirling in 1891 with domeless boiler and the addition of cab side sheets and weatherboard. It was withdrawn in 1898. *LGRP 6197*

53
'F' class 4-4-0 No 11 which was built at Ashford in 1895 and rebuilt to Class F1 in 1913. Note the cylinder for the steam reversing apparatus mounted just ahead of the leading splasher. *LPC 33075*

54

55

56

54
'118' class 2-4-0 No 75 as running in the 1890s after being rebuilt by Stirling with a domeless boiler and the addition of cab side sheets. It was built at Ashford in 1875 and withdrawn in 1904. *LPC 15484*

55
'118' class 2-4-0 No 57 after rebuilding by Stirling. This engine was also built at Ashford in 1875 but it was withdrawn in 1903. *LPC 15564*

56
One of the 25 Class R 0-6-0Ts built at Ashford between 1888 and 1898. This one, No 125 was built in 1895 and withdrawn in 1937. *LGRP 24179*

57
'118' class 2-4-0 No 242 photographed at Charing Cross after rebuilding by Stirling. This engine was one of a batch of 10 built by Dübs in 1866 and which lasted until 1903. *LGRP 21981*

58
Two 'B' class 4-4-0s, Nos 454 and 459, were fitted with Holden's patent oil firing system in 1900 in an attempt to find a cheaper fuel than coal. No 459, which was built by Neilson, Reid & Company in 1898, is seen here as fitted with this apparatus. The experiment was not a success, No 459 being reconverted to coal burning in June 1904 followed by No 454 in February 1905. *LPC 33079*

58

59

60

61

59
Between 1900 and 1904 12 'O' class 0-6-0s were rebuilt with boilers which had deeper fireboxes and this necessitated pitching the boiler higher. No 372 is shown after receiving one of these boilers in September 1902. This engine was sold to the East Kent Railway in 1923 where it became No 6 and, after reboiling with an 'O1' type boiler at Ashford in 1932, it was taken over by British Railways in 1948 and withdrawn the following year. *LPC 33047*

60
'F' class 4-4-0 No 31 in early SECR days before rebuilding to an 'F1' in December 1906. *LPC 33076*

61
'R1' class 0-6-0T No 127 which was rebuilt from Class R in 1914 and is shown in the wartime austerity livery. *RP W5962*

62
'B1' class 4-4-0 No 454. This engine was rebuilt from Class B in 1913 and is shown as later fitted with an extended smokebox. *LPC 15470*

63
Another 'B1' class 4-4-0 with extended smokebox, No 446, which was rebuilt from Class B in 1915. *LPC 15469*

63

64
'F1' class 4-4-0 No 130 photographed at Bricklayers
Arms. It was rebuilt from Class F in 1907 and is shown
as later fitted with an extended smokebox.
LPC 15463

65
'Q' class 0-4-4T No 235 at Victoria in April 1919.
LGRP 14595

66
'Q1' class 0-4-4T No 81 at Bricklayers Arms in May 1920. *LGRP 14599*

67
'F1' class 4-4-0 No 205 at Bricklayers Arms in May 1920, still with a short smokebox. *LGRP 14600*

68

69

70

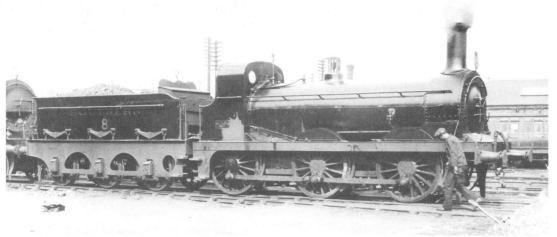

68
Crane tank No 302 which was built by Neilson, Reid & Co in 1881 for service at Folkestone Harbour. It became SR Service Stock No A234S in 1929, returning to normal stock in 1938, when it was renumbered 1302 and which it retained until withdrawal in 1949. *RP W5954*

69
'O' class 0-6-0 No 333 at Slades Green in 1923 as rebuilt in 1911 with square cab and high pitched domeless boiler. It was withdrawn in 1926. *LGRP 14646*

70
'O1' class 0-6-0 No 108 at Slades Green in April 1923. *LGRP 14638*

71
An 'O' class 0-6-0 as running in the mid-1920s as Southern Railway No A8. This engine was never rebuilt as an 'O1' being withdrawn in 1928. *RP W5995*

72
Only two of the 29 Class B 4-4-0s were not rebuilt as Class B1s. One of these is seen here as SR No A34. *RP W6022*

73
'Q' class 0-4-4T No A23 as repainted in Southern green livery. It was withdrawn in 1928. *RP W5973*

74
'B1' class 4-4-0 No A21 as running in SR livery. *RP W6021*

75
An 'R1' class 0-6-0T as running as SR No 1010 after being rebuilt in 1937 with short stovepipe chimney, lowered dome cover and Ross pop safety valves for working on the Canterbury & Whitstable branch. It was withdrawn as BR No 31010 in 1959. *LGRP 4433*

74

75

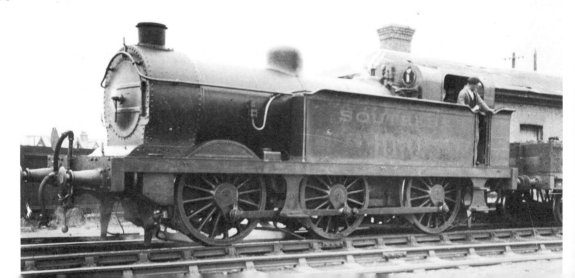

The London Chatham & Dover Railway

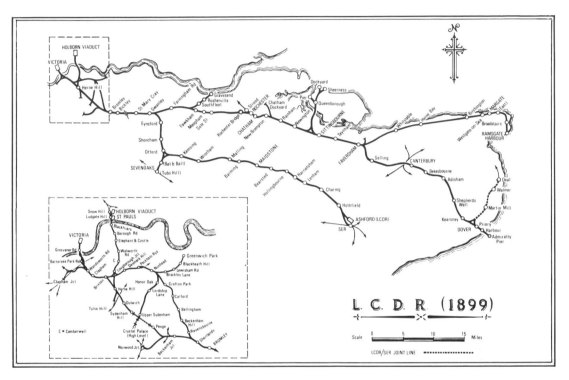

L. C. D. R. (1899)

Scale 0 5 10 15 Miles

LCDR/SER JOINT LINE

By the late 1840s the South Eastern Railway had opened lines from London to the coastal towns of Dover, Whitstable, Margate, Ramsgate and Deal and in July 1849 the final link in the line from London Bridge to Strood was opened but a large part of north Kent was left without railway services. As a result there were several proposals for a direct line through north Kent culminating in the East Kent Railway which was to run from Strood to Canterbury via Rochester and Chatham with branches to the quay at Faversham and Chilham. A rival scheme, known as the Chatham & Canterbury Local Railway, was for a line from Chatham to Chilham but despite the vigorous opposition of the South Eastern the East Kent Railway's bill received Parliamentary sanction on 10 June 1853. The act authorised the East Kent to use the SER's stations at Strood and Canterbury but did not grant running powers over the SER's North Kent line from Gravesend to Strood as had been

hoped for. There was, however, a facilitations clause in the act which required the SER to handle the EKR's traffic between London Bridge and Strood with the same facilities as its own. Further powers were obtained in 1855 for the line to be extended from Canterbury to Dover.

The promoters of the EKR had great difficulty in raising the necessary funds to build the line with the result that construction proceeded slowly and it was not until 25 January 1858 that the first section, which was only a single track from Chatham to Faversham, was publicly opened. On 29 March the section from Chatham to Strood was opened thereby creating an extension of the South Eastern's North Kent line, but despite the facilitations clause in the East Kent's Act, the SER refused to handle any East Kent traffic. The EKR sought to get round this problem by seeking running powers over the SER's line from Strood to Dartford and proposing a new line

41

from there to join up with the West End of London & Crystal Palace Junction Railway thereby gaining access to a new station at Victoria. This scheme, known as the London Extension Bill, was strongly opposed by the South Eastern on the grounds that their North Kent line was already carrying all the traffic it could handle and, as a result the bill was withdrawn. Undeterred, the East Kent then proposed the construction of a new line from Strood to join up with the Bromley & St Mary Cray Railway at Bickley thereby gaining access to a terminus at Battersea through running powers over that line and the West End of London & Crystal Palace Junction Railway. Despite the usual opposition and counter-proposals of the SER, the necessary Parliamentary sanction was obtained in 1858. The same year authority was obtained to extend the line across the Thames from Battersea to a new station at Victoria. The East Kent now extended, on paper at least, from Victoria to Dover so authority was sought from Parliament to change its name to the London Chatham & Dover Railway, this authority being given on 1 August 1859.

In the meantime, construction of the lines continued but was constantly hampered by shortage of money. Considerable cost had already been incurred in building the line from Strood to Faversham, this involving the purchase of costly land and the building of a bridge across the Medway and three tunnels near Chatham. The contractors, Crampton & Co, in order to allow construction to proceed more rapidly, lent the railway company the money to complete the job. On 9 July 1860 the Faversham-Canterbury section was opened, followed on 3 December by the official opening of the Western Extension from Strood (Rochester Bridge) to Bickley thereby allowing the LCDR to work through trains from Victoria to Canterbury. Dover was finally reached with the opening of the line from Canterbury on 22 July 1861, at first to the Town Station, but on 1 November the Harbour station was brought into use with the completion of the Dover Tunnel.

The use of running powers into Victoria Station soon proved most unsatisfactory. The LBSCR ran a frequent service into Victoria and the LCDR had the difficult task of trying to run their trains on already congested lines. The solution was for the LCDR to build its own line and consequently Parliamentary authority was obtained for a line from Stewarts Lane through Herne Hill rejoining the existing main line at Penge Junction near Beckenham. The first section from Stewarts Lane to Herne Hill was opened on 25 August 1862 followed on 1 July 1863 by the final section to Penge Junction, this final section involving the

construction of the 2,200 yard long Penge Tunnel.

In 1860, having failed to secure running powers into London Bridge from the LBSCR, the LCDR sought Parliamentary authority to construct a line northwards from Herne Hill to a terminus at Ludgate Hill on the north bank of the Thames with a connection to Farringdon Street on the Metropolitan Railway. Despite strong opposition, especially from the SER, Parliamentary sanction was eventually received and construction went ahead. The first section to Elephant & Castle was opened on 6 October 1862 but trouble was encountered from the Corporation of London over the design of the bridge over the Thames and the new station at Ludgate Hill was not opened until 1 June 1865 replacing a temporary one used since 21 December 1864.

In 1862 a line from Brixton through Peckham Rye then turning southwards to Crystal Palace was proposed. Part of this line coincided with the proposed South London line of the LBSCR with the result that Parliament ordered that four tracks should be provided over both the LCDR's line from Wandsworth Road to Barrington Road Junction, East Brixton, and the LBSCR's line from there to Cow Lane Junction near Peckham Rye. By this arrangement each company was to have the use of two tracks. The LCDR also received authority to build a line from Cow Lane Junction to Crystal Palace, this being opened on 1 August 1865.

The growth of the railway system in Kent encouraged the promotion of other lines in which the LCDR eventually had an interest. In 1857 an independent company known as the Herne Bay and Faversham Railway proposed a line from Faversham to Herne Bay via Whitstable which, despite strong opposition from the South Eastern, received the necessary approval and was opened to Whitstable on 1 August 1860 and Herne Bay on 13 July 1861. Further powers were obtained and the line was extended to Margate and Ramsgate Harbour in 1863. It was worked by the LCDR, being leased from 1861 and finally taken over in 1871.

A group of businessmen known as the Sevenoaks Company in 1859 obtained Parliamentary sanction for a branch line from Swanley Junction (then known as Sutton-at-Hone) to Sevenoaks (Bat & Ball). It was opened on 2 June 1862 and was extended to the SER's Sevenoaks station (Tubs Hill) in 1869, further extensions being opened to Maidstone on 1 June 1874 and to Ashford on 1 July 1884. This line was also worked by the LCDR, eventually being taken over in 1879.

An important step in the history of the company was taken in 1861 with the appointment of James Staats Forbes to the newly created post of General Manager. At the time of his appointment, Forbes was the Manager of the Dutch Rhenish Railway and, although he spent some time on the company's business before then, it was not until 1 September 1862 that he was able to take over his duties on the LCDR. His character was such that not only did he persuade the directors to pay him the considerable salary for such a small company of £1,500 per annum, but also secured an additional commission which was to be not less than £500 per annum. However, although he was handsomely paid, he worked very hard for the company and was involved in many exchanges with his South Eastern counterpart, Sir Edward Watkin.

In 1862 the government decided to place the contract for the carriage of mails between Dover and Calais in the hands of a single carrier and when the South Eastern turned down the contract the LCDR quickly seized their chance. Arrangements were made with the Dover firm of Jenkins & Churchward to use their steamers and the contract was secured. Later it was agreed that the two companies should carry the mail jointly which they commenced to do from 20 June 1863 and in 1865 co-operation between them was extended even further when a pooling arrangement for the Continental traffic via Dover and Folkestone was introduced.

On 27 February 1865 the company started running the first workmen's trains, between Victoria and Ludgate Hill. It had acquired a reputation as a destroyer of houses in London and, as a gesture of goodwill, had volunteered to run cheap workmen's trains. This concession on the part of the company led to Parliament insisting on the provision of workmen's trains by any railway company that sought authority to do anything involving the demolition of houses.

By 1864 the financial position of the company had become serious and in 1866 it could not meet its obligations. Delays and increased costs incurred in the construction of new lines, particularly the Metropolitan extensions to Ludgate Hill, plus the high rates of interest extorted by the contractors who financed the company had at last taken their toll. J. S. Forbes and W. E. Johnson, the Secretary, were appointed as receivers and a committee was appointed to investigate the running of the company. It was found that many dubious transactions had been entered into, especially those involving their contractors, and the Chairman, Lord Sondes, resigned and was replaced by Lord Harris. As a result, two Arrangement Acts were passed, one in 1867 and one in 1869, to allow the company to raise capital and to provide for the various creditors.

On 18 September 1871 a branch line was opened from Nunhead on the Crystal Palace branch to Blackheath Hill. An extension to Greenwich Park was opened on 1 October 1888 but the line was not a success and it was closed on 1 January 1917.

The Sheerness branch, opened on 19 July 1860, had an extension from Queenborough to a station on Queenborough Pier opened on 15 May 1876 to provide a connection with the steamer service operated to Flushing by the Zeeland Steam Packet Company. This proved a sound investment for many years but the acceleration of the Great Eastern's rival service from Harwich to the Hook of Holland signalled its end. The Great Eastern's route was a shorter one which meant the Queenborough steamers could not compete and consequently in 1911 the service was transferred to Folkestone where it once more became competitive.

Despite the constant rivalry between the LCDR and the SER there were several proposals for their amalgamation. In 1877 the two companies actually got as far as agreeing terms but the agreement came too late for a bill to be presented to Parliament that session and when in February 1878 it was again discussed the LCDR proprietors rejected the idea.

On 15 June 1881 a new line was opened from Dover to Deal which was remarkable in that it was promoted jointly by the LCDR and the SER. The junction at Buckland faced the wrong way for the LCDR's trains to run directly from Deal to London without reversing at Dover, so on 1 July 1882 a loop line was opened to allow through working.

The London suburban traffic had built up rapidly and the use of running powers by the GNR, LSWR and MR caused considerable congestion in and around Ludgate Hill. Two new stations had been opened in 1874, one at Holborn Viaduct and one at Snow Hill, but the original bridge over the Thames had become a bottleneck so in 1886 a new bridge carrying seven tracks was built together with a new station, St Pauls.

The 'Continental Agreement' of 1865 whereby the LCDR and the SER had agreed to pool the receipts for the Continental traffic via Dover and Folkestone was the cause of serious trouble between the two companies in 1886 which resulted in protracted action in the law courts. The South Eastern claimed that the agreement only applied to Folkestone and Folkestone Harbour stations and not to the neighbouring stations of Cheriton Arch (renamed Radnor Park in September 1886) and Shorncliffe Camp, an interpretation which was disputed by the LCDR. Also in dispute were the receipts for the Queenborough traffic which the South Eastern complained was outside the terms of the agreement since it was not situated on the coast between Margate and Hastings. The dispute was dragged backwards and forwards through the courts eventually reaching the House of Lords which in 1890 finally ruled in favour of the LCDR, compensation of £85,000 being awarded against the South Eastern.

On 1 July 1892 a new line known as the Catford Loop was opened from Nunhead to Shortlands which gave an alternative route into the City avoiding the Penge Tunnel. Although it was owned by a local company, it was worked by the LCDR and absorbed by them in 1896.

After the settlement of the dispute over the 'Continental Agreement' in 1890 relations with the SER gradually improved. Negotiations were started with the South Eastern and in 1898 agreement for a working union of the two companies was finally reached whereby each company was to retain its legal and financial identity but for engineering and operating matters they were to be worked as one company.

76

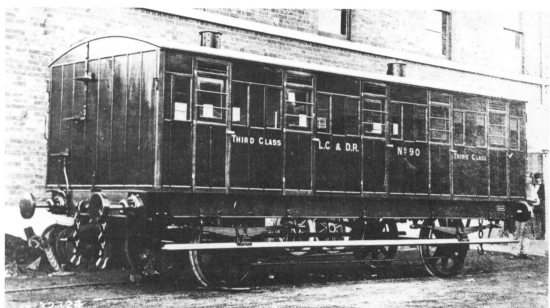

77

76
This four-wheeled third, No 90, with five compartments
was built by the Gloucester Railway Carriage & Wagon
Company in May 1862. Its body was 25ft 0in long and
8ft 6in wide and it was withdrawn in January 1884.
LPC 32324

77
'Europa' class 2-4-0 No 54 *Asia* passing St Mary Cray
during the 1880s. *LGRP 17910*

78
'Enigma' class 2-4-0 No 52 piloting a 4-4-0 through
Swanley Junction with a passenger train.
LGRP 21648

79
'M3' class 4-4-0 No 16 near Bickley in 1898 with a
train of seven vehicles which includes two bogie
coaches. *LGRP 21260*

79

80
Another view near Bickley in 1898, this time showing
'M3' No 13 with a train which includes four bogie
vehicles. *LGRP 21261*

81
St Mary Cray station was on the section of the line from
Bickley to Rochester Bridge (Strood) which was opened
on 3 December 1860. It is pictured here about 1910.
LPC 39058

82
Ramsgate (C&D) was opened with the line from Herne
Bay to Ramsgate on 5 October 1863. In July 1899 its

name was altered to Ramsgate Harbour to avoid
confusion with the South Eastern's station and it was
closed on 2 July 1926 following improvements in the
Ramsgate area which included the opening of two new
stations. It is pictured here in 1924. *LGRP 8897*

83
'Europa' class 2-4-0 No 54 with a down express near
Bickley in 1898. *LGRP 15137*

84
'M3' class 4-4-0 No 12 with a Dover boat express near
Bickley in 1898. *LGRP 17945*

82

83

84

85
'M3' class 4-4-0 No 650 passing Swanley Junction with a passenger train in 1903. This engine was one of a batch of six built by the Vulcan Foundry in 1891, the only ones of the class not to be built at Longhedge. It was originally LCDR No 191 and it was withdrawn in December 1926 as SR No A650. *LGRP 21327*

86
'Adrian' class 0-6-0 No 588 passing St Mary Cray with a passenger train about 1903. No 588 was built in 1866 and named *Vespasian* but it was later given the number 129 and the name was removed. It is shown here after reboilering by Kirtley in 1890 and with its SECR number. *LGRP 21399*

87
'M3' class 4-4-0 No 462 (formerly LCDR No 3) passing Swanley Junction with a passenger train in the early years of the century. *LGRP 21455*

88
Canterbury East station and yard as it was in 1924. It was opened on 9 July 1860 when the line to Faversham was opened, in LCDR days being known simply as Canterbury. In July 1899 it was renamed Canterbury East to avoid confusion with the South Eastern's station. *LGRP 8895*

89
'M1' class 4-4-0 No 636 passing Swanley Junction with a passenger train about 1910. This engine was built at Longhedge in 1881 as LCDR No 177 and withdrawn in May 1912. *LGRP 21543*

90
'M3' class 4-4-0 No 475
(formerly LCDR No 16) on a
Faversham to Dover stopping
train. *LPC 23148*

91
Dover was reached on
22 July 1861 when the line
from Canterbury was opened.
At first the station was known as
Dover Town but it was renamed
Dover Priory in July 1863.
This view was taken in 1931.
LGRP 8959

91

92
On 1 November 1861 the
line was extended from the
Town station to Dover Harbour
which is pictured here in 1925.
After the opening of the Marine
station in 1915 the number
of trains stopping at the Harbour
station was gradually reduced
until it was finally closed on
10 July 1927. *LGRP 8912*

92

London Chatham & Dover Locomotives

The responsibility for the East Kent Railway's earliest locomotives rested with the company's engineer, Joseph Cubitt, although the contractor for the line, T. R. Crampton, exerted considerable influence, the first locomotives being of his design. These were a class of six 4-4-0 saddle tanks ordered from R. & W. Hawthorn in 1857 of which only the first two, *Lake* and *Sondes*, had been delivered in time for the opening of the first section of the line from Chatham to Faversham on 25 January 1858. Although these engines had more than sufficient power for hauling the lightly loaded early trains, they were heavy on coke and very troublesome performers, frequently breaking down. Their unreliability together with the expected opening of further lines necessitated the acquisition of more engines and preferably cheap ones so in May 1860 two 6ft 0in singles were purchased secondhand from R. & W. Hawthorn and put to work on main line passsenger trains. These were followed by a small six-coupled tender engine named *Swale*, purchased from Brotherhood of Chippenham, and an 0-4-0 wing tank named *Magnus* purchased from R. & W. Hawthorn, both for working the newly opened branch from Sittingbourne to Sheerness.

In the meantime, it had been decided to appoint a proper Locomotive Superintendent, the man chosen, William Martley, taking up his duties on 5 April 1860. Martley was an experienced locomotive engineer who came to the LCDR from the Great Western where he had been a District Locomotive Superintendent. His new job must have been a daunting one: he was not only hampered by the continual financial crises which beset the company but also had to contend with the inadequate early locomotives acquired by Cubitt and with a Board influenced by Crampton. In addition to all this he was responsible for the carriage, wagon, running and marine departments!

In June 1860 the Board agreed to the purchase of two 0-6-0 goods engines which had been offered by R. & W. Hawthorn. They had been hired out to various contractors by the makers but nevertheless they were only 10 months old when they arrived in August 1860.

The purchase of five passenger, 24 general purpose and eight goods engines was authorised in July 1860 but until these arrived in 1861/62 the acquisition of miscellaneous engines continued. In 1860/61 there arrived four 4-4-0 tender engines with 5ft 0in coupled wheels which had been built by Stephenson for the Smyrna & Aidin railway in Turkey and had been left on the maker's hands. The first engine *Aeolus* arrived in September 1860 and worked the first through train from Strood to Victoria on 3 December by which time a serious shortage of locomotives had only been avoided by the hire of six 'Small Hawthorn' singles from the GNR and the purchase of three old 2-2-0s from the LNWR. The latter proved next to useless and within a year all three were out of service.

An unusual agreement was made with the Glasgow & South Western Railway in 1860 whereby the LCDR was allowed to purchase two engines from a batch of 20 being built for the Scottish company by Sharp, Stewart. They were 0-4-2 tender engines designed by Patrick Stirling and they arrived on the LCDR in August 1861 where they were named *Brigand* and *Corsair*.

After J. S. Forbes was appointed general manager he brought to the attention of the company six Sharp, Stewart 2-4-0s which were stored out of use by the Dutch Rhenish railway, the company he had left to join the LCDR. Their purchase was arranged and they entered service between August and October 1861 at the same time as the first of the new locomotives ordered in July 1860. These were the first few of the 24 general purposes engines which were inside-framed 4-4-0 Cramptons with outside cylinders and Cudworth coal-burning fireboxes. Their performance was particularly poor and all were rebuilt between 1862 and 1865, all except two as 2-4-0s.

The order for the eight goods engines in July 1860 was eventually increased to 14, six from Sharp, Stewart and eight from R. Stephenson, delivery being made between September 1861 and December 1862. They were known as the

'Acis' class and were double-framed 0-6-0s with 5ft 0in wheels and Cudworth coal-burning fireboxes although they were rebuilt with conventional fireboxes with brick arches between 1870 and 1874. They were powerful engines and worked most of the company's main line goods services.

Considerable delay was experienced with the delivery of the five passenger engines ordered in July 1860 and consequently they did not arrive until the spring of 1862. They were unconventional locomotives designed by Crampton and featured a single pair of driving wheels which were driven by coupling rods connected to a crankshaft mounted ahead of the driving axle. Although they performed much better than most Cramptons, it was a relatively easy job to convert them to 4-4-0s by substituting a pair of driving wheels for the crankshaft, this alteration being made to all five engines in 1863/64. Much better engines were thereby produced and they successfully worked the boat trains for the next 10 years or so.

The new locomotive and carriage works at Longhedge was brought into use in 1862, built on land purchased from Long Hedge Farm near Battersea. At first the works was used for repairs and for rebuilding the unsatisfactory early locomotives and it was not until 1869 that the first new engine to be built there was completed.

The first engines of Martley's design were delivered by the makers, Sharp, Stewart & Co, in the autumn of 1862. In contrast to the unusual locomotives designed by Crampton, they were fairly conventional double-framed 2-4-0s, although they did have Cudworth coal-burning fireboxes. These six engines, which were known as the 'Dawn' class, were joined the following year by a further six, known as the 'Bluebell' class, which were generally similar but had a boiler which was 3in smaller in diameter and 6in longer.

The constant turning of tender engines caused a great deal of congestion in the London area so in an attempt to alleviate this problem Martley ordered six 2-4-0 side tanks from R. & W. Hawthorn for use on short distance trains. They were delivered in the summer of 1863 and for the next 10 years worked suburban trains in the London area.

In the summer of 1865 Peto, Brassey & Betts delivered six 2-4-0 tender engines with double frames and Cudworth coal-burning fireboxes, the first engine of which was named *Reindeer*. Later, Kirtley numbered them 44 to 49 and reboilered them in 1881-83.

The opening of the extensions in the London area in the early 1860s necessitated the provision of suitable locomotives, so in 1866 14 0-4-2 well tanks were delivered by Neilson. They were very similar to Archibald Sturrock's Great Northern engines introduced the previous year, Sturrock agreeing to the use of his design, and because of their Scottish names they were known as 'Scotchmen'. Kirtley numbered them 81 to 94 in the 1870s and between 1880 and 1892 rebuilt them all with his own type of boiler, withdrawal taking place between 1904 and 1909.

Following the success of the 'Acis' class 0-6-0s, six similar engines were built by John Fowler in 1866 and known as the 'Adrian' class. Kirtley numbered them 127 to 132 in the 1870s and they were withdrawn between 1907 and 1910.

In 1869/70 three 2-4-0 passenger tender engines were built at Longhedge Works, the first engine bearing the name *Enigma*. They were generally similar to the 'Reindeer' class but *Enigma* had 6ft 0in coupled wheels instead of 6ft 6in and the other two engines, *Mermaid* and *Lothair*, had fireboxes with brick arches. The Cudworth firebox on *Enigma* was replaced with a brick arch firebox in 1874 and in 1882 all three were rebuilt with Kirtley boilers.

When further locomotives were required to cope with the continual growth of suburban traffic in the London area the Great Northern was again turned to for help. As a result, six 0-4-2 well tanks based on Stirling's GN design were built by Neilson in 1873. They were known as the 'Large Scotchmen' and were later numbered 95 to 100.

Two 0-6-0 tender engines with inside frames and 4ft 6½in wheels were purchased from Sharp, Stewart in 1873 and were given the names *Huz* and *Buz*, later receiving Nos 133 and 134 respectively. Both were rebuilt with new boilers in 1888 and both lasted until 1901.

The third new class of locomotive to appear in 1873 was the four 2-4-0 tender engines built in that year by Sharp, Stewart for working the continental mail trains. They had 6ft 6in coupled wheels, double frames and conventional fireboxes with brick arches and in 1875 they were numbered 53 to 56 — two further engines, Nos 57 and 58, being completed at Longhedge the following year. They gave good service on the boat trains for many years ending their days on local passenger or pilot duties and being withdrawn between 1907 and 1909.

On 6 February 1874 William Martley died and the following month William Kirtley was appointed Locomotive Superintendent in his place. Kirtley's first design was the 'A' class 0-4-4T built in 1875 for working the ever increasing London suburban traffic. They had 5ft 3in coupled wheels and they were fitted with condensing apparatus, a total of 18 being built, half each by Neilson and the Vulcan Foundry. No 111 (as SECR No 570) was withdrawn after an

Onyx, one of the six Sharp, Stewart 2-4-0s purchased from the Dutch Rhenish railway in 1861, all of which were converted to tank engines at Longhedge in 1864/65. *LPC 32317*

accident in 1915 but the remaining 17 engines all entered Southern Railway stock in 1923. However, electrification soon rendered them redundant and all had gone by 1926.

Kirtley's next design was introduced in 1876, six 0-6-0 goods tender engines known as the 'B' class. They were built by Dübs and had 4ft 10in wheels and inside frames and were numbered 135-140. The following year six similar engines, Nos 151 to 156, known as the 'B1' class, were built by Neilson. Kirtley's first express passenger engines, the six 'M' class 4-4-0s Nos 157 to 162, were built by Neilson in 1877. They proved successful and in 1880/81 four similar engines, Nos 175 to 178 known as the 'M1' class, were built at Longhedge. The six 'Ms' were all withdrawn between 1911 and 1914 but No 176 (as SECR No 635) of Class M1 lasted until 1923.

The LCDR had always suffered from a shortage of suitable shunting engines which meant that these duties often had to be performed by large wheeled tender engines. Despite complaints it was not until 1879 that suitable engines were acquired and then only two were built. These two engines, Nos 141 and 142, were 0-6-0 side tanks with 4ft 6in wheels built at Longhedge Works and known as the 'T' class. Although they were successful engines it was another 10 years before any further engines were built, construction then continuing until 1893 when the class had been increased to 10. All 10 engines entered SR stock in 1923 and three lasted long enough to be taken over by BR, the last survivor being withdrawn in 1951.

In 1880 a class of 12 0-4-4 side tank engines was built by Kitson for suburban traffic. These engines, Nos 163 to 174, were known as the 'A1'

class and were based on the successful 'A' class of 1875 but with 5ft 7in coupled wheels. They were as successful as the 'A' class and all entered SR stock in 1923 but they suffered the same fate as the earlier class and all had gone by 1926. In 1883/84 six similar engines, the 'A2' class, were built by Stephenson.

It had been intended to build two further engines of the 'M1' class 4-4-0s, Nos 179 and 180, but completion had been delayed by a fire at Longhedge Works. More passenger engines were urgently required and, since the work could not be carried out at Longhedge in the near future, tenders were sought from private manufacturers with the result that six engines, Nos 181 to 186, were supplied by Dübs in early 1884. They were known as the 'M2' class and they were generally similar to their predecessors also having inside frames and cylinders and 6ft 6in coupled wheels. The two delayed engines, Nos 179 and 180, were eventually completed at Longhedge late in 1885.

During the late 1880s increases in traffic and loads made it increasingly difficult for the older passenger engines to cope. There was therefore a need for new, more powerful engines so in 1891 Kirtley introduced his 'M3' class 4-4-0s, the first six engines, Nos 187 to 192, being built by the Vulcan Foundry. Like the earlier 4-4-0s they had 6ft 6in coupled wheels but the cylinders were enlarged from $17\frac{1}{2}$in to 18in×26in, the boiler pressure was increased from 140 to 150lb/sq in and the boilers were 2in longer. These changes were relatively small but they were obviously important for the new engines were a great improvement on the earlier 4-4-0s. A further 20 engines were built at Longhedge from 1892 until 1901 and they joined the first six in working the company's most important trains. All 26 entered SR stock in 1923 but they were all withdrawn between 1925 and 1928.

Late in 1891 Sharp, Stewart delivered 18 0-4-4 side tank engines, 'R' class Nos 199 to 216, which were built for working the faster sub-urban services in the London area. Commencing in 1912 they were all rebuilt with boilers of the type fitted to the later 'H' class and from 1917 all except two were fitted with apparatus for working auto-trains. Consequently, when electrification made them redundant in the London area in the 1920s, work was found for them on local trains in other parts of the system. Three were withdrawn in 1940 but the rest entered BR stock in 1948 and the last two were not withdrawn until 1955.

The last new class to be introduced before the formation of the Managing Committee in 1899 was the 'B2' class of six 0-6-0 goods tender engines built by the Vulcan Foundry in 1891. They were an improved version of the 'B1s' with larger cylinders and they were numbered 193 to 198. One engine was rebuilt in 1910 with an 'H' class boiler, the intention being to similarly rebuild the whole class, but because of a shortage of new boilers only one more was so equipped and the remaining four engines in 1914/15 received secondhand boilers bought from the GNR. They were all withdrawn between 1929 and 1933.

When, in 1898, the LCDR and the SER decided to form a working union it was also decided that each company's locomotive superintendent should be retired and one man appointed in their place. Accordingly, on 27 September 1898 Harry S. Wainwright, the South Eastern's Carriage & Wagon Superintendent, was appointed to the new post of Locomotive, Carriage & Wagon Superintendent and on 31 December William Kirtley retired.

94
One of the 24 general purpose engines built in 1861/62 and known as the 'Tiger' class. This one, *Tiger*, was one of six built by Slaughter, Gruning & Co, and is shown as running about 1870 after being rebuilt to a 2-4-0 but still retaining its Cudworth coal-burning firebox. *LPC 32318*

95
'Echo' class 4-4-0 *Sylph* after conversion from a Crampton 4-2-0 in 1864 but still retaining its Cudworth coal-burning firebox which was replaced by one with a brick arch in 1872. It was later given the number 31 and was withdrawn in 1902 as SECR No 490. *LPC 32316*

96
Jura, one of the 14 'Scotchmen' built by Neilson & Co in 1866 and based on Archibald Sturrock's Great Northern design. It was later numbered 83 and was withdrawn in 1906 as SECR No 542A. *LPC 32342*

97
'Tiger' class 2-4-0 *Swallow* as running in the 1870s with conventional brick arch firebox and reduced rear overhang. *LPC 15301*

94

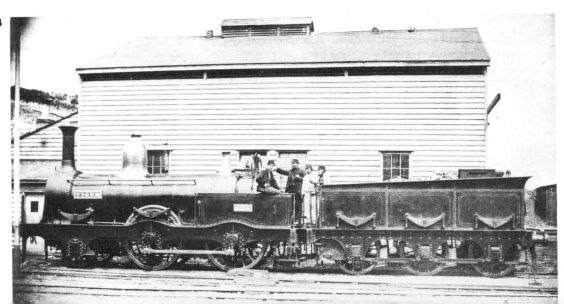

95

96

97

98

98
Swale, an 0-6-0ST which was purchased from Brotherhood of Cheltenham as an 0-6-0 tender engine in 1860 and rebuilt to a saddle tank in 1865. It was given the number 141 and its name removed in 1875, renumbered 141A in 1879 and withdrawn in 1881. *LPC 15336*

99
'Aeolus' class 2-4-0T *Bacchus* as rebuilt in 1872 from one of the 4-4-0Ts built as tender engines by Robert Stephenson & Co to an order by the Turkish Smyrna & Aidin railway. *LPC 32340*

100
'Echo' class 4-4-0 No 28 (formerly *Coquette*) as

running about 1880 after receiving a conventional brick arch firebox. It was withdrawn in 1906 as SECR No 487A. *LPC 23137*

101
'Reindeer' class 2-4-0 *Elk*, one of a class of six engines built in 1865 by Peto, Brassey & Betts. It is shown as running from 1875 to 1881 with an early Kirtley cab and brick arch firebox. *LPC 15326*

102
No 153 of Class B1, six of which were built by Neilson & Co in 1877. It became SECR No 612 and was one of two engines of this class to enter Southern Railway stock in 1923 although it was withdrawn the same year. *LPC 32312*

99

103
'A2' class 0-4-4T No 80 at Finsbury Park, GNR.
LGRP 21661

104
Two 0-6-0 tender engines were purchased from the makers, R. & W. Hawthorn & Co, in 1860 and named *Hercules* and *Ajax*. In 1865 both were rebuilt as saddle tanks and later the names were removed and they received the numbers 143 and 144. No 143 (formerly *Hercules*) is seen here after reboilering by Kirtley in 1878. Both engines were withdrawn in 1895.
LPC 32303

105
The six unsuccessful Crampton 4-4-0Ts of the 'Sondes'

class were all rebuilt as conventional 2-4-0Ts in 1865, although little of the original engines remained. No 59 (formerly *Sondes*) is shown after rebuilding with a Kirtley boiler in 1878. It was withdrawn as SECR No 518 in 1909. *LPC 15630*

106
'Europa' class 2-4-0 No 54 *Asia* at Wandsworth Road in the 1880s. It was one of four of this class built by Sharp, Stewart & Co in 1873. *LPC 32346*

107
'Enigma' class 2-4-0 No 50 (formerly *Enigma*) after rebuilding by Kirtley with a new boiler in 1882. It was withdrawn as SECR No 509 in 1906. *LPC 15306*

105

106

107

108

109

110

108
'Dawn' class 2-4-0 No 34 *Herald* as running in the
1880s after having its coupled wheelbase lengthened.
LPC 15325

109
'M' class 4-4-0 No 162, one of six engines of this class,
all of which were built by Neilson & Co in 1877.
No 162 became SECR No 621 and was withdrawn in
1911. *LPC 15328*

110
Only four engines of the 'M1' class were built, all at
Longhedge in 1880/81. No 176 illustrated became
SECR No 635 and was the only engine of the class to
be taken over by the Southern Railway but was
withdrawn soon after. *LPC 15310*

111
'Acis' class 0-6-0 No 116 one of a batch of six built by
Sharp, Stewart & Co in 1861/62. No 116 was
originally named *Fortuna* and is shown after reboilering
by Kirtley in 1884. It became SECR No 575 and was
withdrawn in 1908, by then on the Duplicate List as
No 575A. *LPC 15320*

112
'T' class 0-6-0T No 149 which was the third engine of
the class to be built, in 1889, 10 years after the first
two, Nos 141 and 142. It became SECR No 608 and
was withdrawn in 1936 as SR No 1608. *LPC 15318*

112

113

114

115

113
No 199, the first of the 18 Class R 0-4-4Ts, all of which
were built by Sharp, Stewart & Co in 1891. Between
1912 and 1937 they were all reboilered with H class
boilers and between 1920 and 1925 all had their
condensing gear removed. No 199 was withdrawn in
1952 as BR No 31658. *LGRP 16122*

114
'B' class 0-6-0 No 195, one of a class of six engines
built by the Vulcan Foundry in 1891. This engine
became SECR No 654 and was one of the four engines
of this class to be fitted (in 1914/15) with secondhand
boilers bought from the Great Northern Railway. It was
withdrawn in 1933 as SR No A654. *LGRP 21986*

115
No 99 *Mona*, one of the six 'Large Scotchmen', all of

which were built by Neilson & Co in 1873, their design
being based on Patrick Stirling's Great Northern class
of 0-4-2WTs. No 99 was withdrawn in 1910 as SECR
No 558. *LPC 32344*

116
'Adrian' class 0-6-0 No 131 which was built in 1866
by John Fowler & Co, one of a class of six. It was
named *Pertinax* when built and is shown here after
reboilering by Kirtley in 1890. It was withdrawn in
1910 as SECR No 590A. *LGRP 4192*

117
0-4-2WT No 88, one of the 'Scotchmen', after
reboilering by Kirtley in 1888. It was originally named
Clyde and was withdrawn in 1908 as SECR No 547.
LGRP 4443

118

119

120

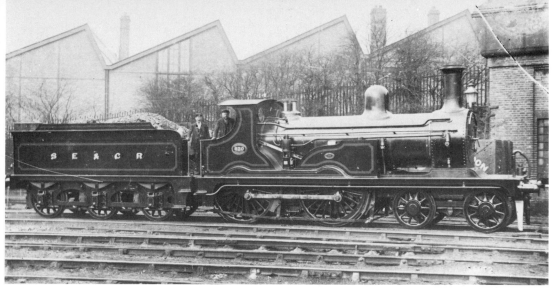

118
'Bluebell' class 2-4-0 No 41 (formerly *Verbena*) after reboilering by Kirtley in 1882. *LPC 32347*

119
'Acis' class 0-6-0 No 126, one of a batch of eight built by Robert Stephenson & Co in 1862. This engine, which was originally named *Thisbe*, is shown after reboilering by Kirtley in 1881. *LPC 23134*

120
'M3' class 4-4-0 No 25 photographed at Ramsgate Sands. *LGRP 28529*

121
'M' class 4-4-0 No 161 after repainting in the Wainwright lined green livery and renumbering 620. It was withdrawn in 1911. *LPC 33073.*

122
An 'Echo' class 4-4-0 as running in early SECR days repainted in Wainwright lined green livery and renumbered 488. It became No 488A on the Duplicate List in September 1902, withdrawal taking place in July 1903. *LGRP 18242*

123

124

125

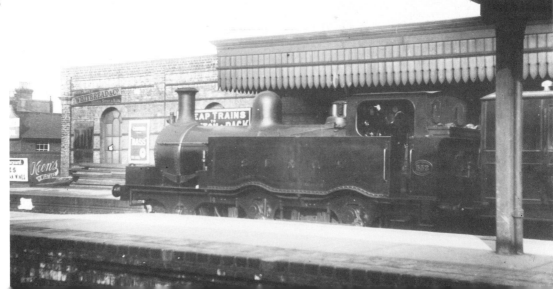

123
Another view taken in early SECR days of an LCDR
2-4-0 in Wainwright lined green livery, this one being
'Dawn' No 492, which was placed on the Duplicate List
as No 492A in April 1903 and withdrawn in December
1904. *LGRP 18273*

124
'Tiger' class 2-4-0 No 470, also in Wainwright lined
green livery. *LGRP 18250*

125
'Aeolus' class 2-4-0T No 532 as running in its final
years after reboilering by Kirtley in 1888. It became

No 532A in July 1905 and was condemned in April
1906. *LGRP 28540*

126
'A2' class 0-4-4T No 536 at Enfield, GNR, one of a
class of six engines built by Robert Stephenson & Co in
1883/84. *LPC 15474*

127
'T' class 0-6-0T No 600 at Battersea in October 1920.
Originally LCDR No 141, it was the first engine of the
class, built in 1879 and withdrawn in 1936 as SR
No 1600. *LGRP 14607*

128
'A1' class 0-4-4T No 626 at Battersea in September 1921 after having its condensing gear removed. It was withdrawn in 1926 as SR No A626. *LGRP 14620*

129
'A' class 0-4-4T No 560 at Battersea in June 1923. This engine was originally LCDR No 101 and was the first engine of the 'A' class to be built, being the first of a batch of nine built by Neilson & Co in 1875. Its condensing gear was removed in 1922 and it was withdrawn in 1925, still in SECR livery. *LGRP 14648*

129

130
'M3' class 4-4-0 No 473 at Battersea in May 1924.
LGRP 14652

131
'M3' class 4-4-0 No A484 as running about 1925 in
Southern Railway green livery. It was withdrawn in
1926.   *RP W6040*

The South Eastern & Chatham Railway

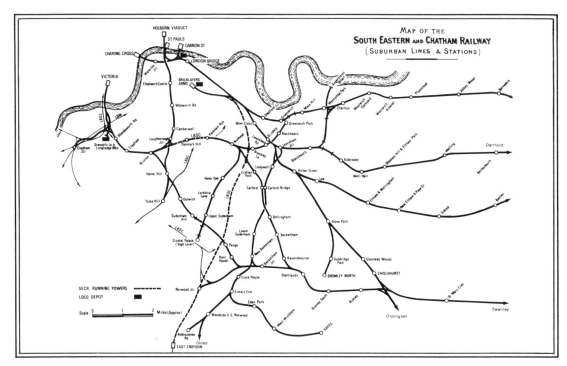

MAP OF THE
SOUTH EASTERN AND CHATHAM RAILWAY
(SUBURBAN LINES & STATIONS)

On 1 January 1899 the South Eastern and London Chatham & Dover railways started to operate under the terms of their agreement of the previous year. They did not amalgamate in the usual way but instead formed a working union whereby they were to be operated as a single railway under the control of a Managing Committee, the Chairman of which was the SER's Chairman with the LCDR's Chairman as his deputy. This arrangement came into operation in advance of Parliamentary sanction which was not received until 1 August 1899. Under the terms of the agreement the net receipts were to be divided so that the SER was to receive 59% with the remaining 41% going to the LCDR.

Much was necessary to improve the two companies. The track was in poor condition after years of neglect and they were both unpopular with the travelling public; timekeeping was poor and much of the coaching stock was in a deplor-

able condition, some of it dating from the 1850s. The South Eastern had started to improve their passenger stock and during the 1890s produced some reasonable coaches but shortage of money meant that many of the older vehicles were kept in service. The SECR built coaches which were a great improvement on their predecessors but compartment stock without connecting corridors was persisted with until 1921, few corridor coaches being produced before then.

On 4 June 1901 a branch line from Purley to Tattenham Corner was opened throughout. Until then the Epsom race traffic had been monopolised by the LSWR and LBSCR but their stations were further from the racecourse than the new SECR one at Tattenham Corner and this enabled the SECR to capture most of the race traffic.

Another advantage was gained over the LBSCR when, on 1 June 1902, a branch line was opened from a new junction at Crowhurst, near Hastings, to the popular resort of Bexhill. The distance to Bexhill over the new route was 11 miles less from Cannon Street than the LBSCR's route from Victoria.

Important improvements were made in the London area where heavy traffic congestion was a constant problem. The widening of the South Eastern line between London Bridge and New Cross was completed in 1902 and extended as far as Orpington on 18 June 1905. Connecting loops were also put in between the SER and the LCDR main lines.

In 1905 improvements to the pier station at Folkestone Harbour were completed. The existing station had become inadequate for handling boat trains of bogie stock so in 1897 the South Eastern had decided to extend the pier and improve the station facilities. The new steamer berths provided enabled the new turbine steamers being built for the comapny to berth at any state of the tide, the boat trains then running alongside the steamers.

A serious accident befell the company on 5 December 1905 when part of the roof of Charing Cross station collapsed, the cause of which was the breaking of a tie rod brought about by a flaw in the original welding. Thankfully, there were few people around at 3.40pm when the collapse occurred and there were few casualties. The station was closed until 19 March 1906 but the existence of the company's other termini at Cannon Street, Victoria and St Pauls, to which the Charing Cross trains could be diverted, meant that the inconvenience suffered was less than might otherwise have been the case.

In the early years of the century the Admiralty was improving its naval facilities at Dover. The railway facilities were poor and it was therefore decided to build a new station on reclaimed land adjacent to the Admiralty Pier. Work commenced in 1910 and was not completed until 1914 but by this time World War 1 had broken out and the new station, known as Dover Marine, was opened for military traffic only on 2 January 1915. The war meant that a large volume of military traffic was dealt with at Dover and the improved facilities there were an important national asset.

When Britain entered World War 1 in August 1914, the SECR was at once called upon to deal with the flood of refugees arriving from the continent. This reached a peak in October when Antwerp and Ostend were occupied by the Germans, 36,000 refugees arriving in one week and 6,000 on one day alone. Dover was taken over by the Government for military use and three of the SECR's latest turbine steamers were converted to seaplane carriers for use by the Royal Navy. The war, of course, created a tremendous increase in traffic, especially in view of the fact that Woolwich Arsenal was served by the SECR. Trainloads of equipment for the forces on the continent were leaving Woolwich for the ports and a constant supply of materials was arriving there. In 1913 only about a quarter of the company's traffic had been goods and this was handled by the old system which was customary throughout much of the country. By this method goods trains were run as and when they were required but the tremendous increase in goods traffic after the outbreak of war quickly led to intolerable congestion. Changes in operating practices therefore became an urgent necessity with the result that on the routes from London to the channel ports the timetable was divided into 'paths' which could be allocated to special trains as required.

On 19 December 1915 a serious landslip occurred in Folkestone Warren between the Martello and Abbotscliff tunnels. Owing to the vigilance of a watchman, who succeeded in stopping a train just after it had emerged from the Martello Tunnel, there were no casualties but the damage to the line was such that it was abandoned for the duration of the war. It was not reopened until 11 August 1919 during which period all traffic to Dover had to use the LCDR route.

By this time axle loads of locomotives and rolling stock using the bridges leading into Charing Cross and Cannon Street stations had trebled since they were built in the 1860s. Furthermore, the sheer volume of traffic carried was constantly increasing and electrification was under consideration so the decision was taken to strengthen the bridges, the work at Cannon Street taking $4\frac{1}{2}$ years to complete.

Considerable improvements in the working of trains in the London area were effected in 1922 by the introduction of parallel working. The constant growth of suburban traffic inevitably caused congestion, particularly in the approaches to Cannon Street, Charing Cross and London Bridge, and this was alleviated by rearranging the timetable so that trains travelling parallel to each other made simultaneous parallel moves over junctions. The new system was at first tried out during the morning rush period and after a successful trial it was introduced during the evening rush period, enjoying equal success.

On 1 January 1923 the SECR became part of the Southern Railway which was formed on that day as a result of the Railways Act of 1921. Although the new Chairman, Sir Hugh Drummond, and the new General Manager, Sir Herbert Walker, were both formerly LSWR men, SECR men were appointed to many senior positions, especially in the locomotive department where

R. E. L. Maunsell became the Chief Mechanical Engineer.

The work of the Managing Committee was far from complete by 1923 but since its formation in 1899, and despite more than four years of war, tremendous improvements had been made in the two companies which 25 years earlier, to quote Cosmo Bonsor, Chairman throughout this period, 'were a standing joke with the clown of the pantomime and with the comic gentlemen in the Music Halls'.

132

A Dover boat express passing Grove Park in 1901 headed by 'D' class 4-4-0 No 726 which was then brand new. *LGRP 21252*

133

'D' class 4-4-0 No 738 passing St Mary Cray with an express about 1903. *LGRP 21378*

134

An up boat express approaching Shakespeare Cliff near Dover in 1903 headed by 'D' class No 728. Note the contractors' material in the foreground which was being used in connection with the Harbour extension. *LGRP 21330*

135

No 177, one of the two Bogie First Saloons built in 1900. In 1907 it was converted to an Invalid Saloon, eventually becoming SR No 7913, and in 1936 it was sold to the Longmoor Military Railway. Later it was preserved by the Transport Trust and transferred to the Severn Valley Railway. *LPC 33130*

136

Whyteleafe station on the Caterham branch which was opened on 1 January 1900. *LGRP 19997*

137

138

139

137
A 15-coach train near Honor Oak on the Crystal Palace
Branch hauled by 'H' class 0-4-4T No 162.
LPC 33123

138
A branch line was opened from Crowhurst to Bexhill on
1 June 1902 thereby breaking the LBSCR's monopoly
of the Bexhill traffic. Bexhill station was renamed
Bexhill West on 9 July 1923 and is seen here in 1931.
LGRP 8978

139
'C' class 0-6-0 No 573 with a passenger train of nine
six-wheelers and one bogie coach. *LPC 33065*

140
A passenger train near St Mary Cray headed by 'G'
class 4-4-0 No 676. *RP T7992*

141
'D' class 4-4-0 No 730 emerging from Shakespeare
Cliff Tunnel with a down express. *LGRP 21425*

142
Elmstead Woods station photographed about 1910. It was opened on 1 July 1904 as Elmstead and renamed on 1 October 1908. *LPC 39056*

143
In May 1912 'P' class 0-6-0T No 325 was equipped for push and pull working for the service between Nunhead and Greenwich Park. It is seen here at Greenwich Park in July 1912 with Bogie Composite No 2713 and Bogie Third Brake No 3396. *LPC 15881*

144
'E' class 4-4-0 No 157 with an up boat express near Folkestone in June 1914. *LPC 23144*

145
A Cannon Street-Ramsgate train near Broadstairs headed by 'D' class 4-4-0 No 732 in wartime austerity livery. *RP T6043*

146
'H' class 0-4-4T No 517 with a passenger train of 13 vehicles about 1921. *LGRP 28515*

143

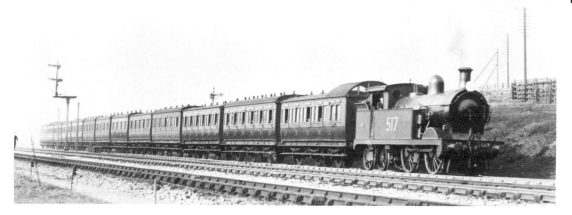

147
'N' class 2-6-0 No 813 with a fitted goods train about 1921 *LGRP 28525*

148
'J' class 0-6-4T No 207 with a fitted goods train about 1921. *LGRP 28505*

149
'E1' class 4-4-0 No 506 with a down train which includes two Pullman cars near Chelsfield in 1922. *LGRP 16620*

150
A down milk train near Purley headed by 'C' class 0-6-0 No 721 which had both vacuum and Westinghouse brake equipment. *RP T6044*

151
'C' class 0-6-0 No 54 passing Chelsfield with a down goods train in 1922. *LGRP 16635*

152
A down Hastings express near Chelsfield in 1922 hauled by 'L' class No 776. *LGRP 16636*

153
A down Continental boat express, which includes three Pullman cars, near Chelsfield in 1922 hauled by 'D1' class No 489. *LGRP 16640*

154
'J' class 0-6-4T No 614 passing Chelsfield with a down passenger train for Sevenoaks about 1922.
LGRP 16627

155
'C' class 0-6-0 No 590 passing Chelsfield with an up goods train about 1923. *LGRP 16648*

156
A photograph of 'H' class 0-4-4T No 321 with an up passenger train from Sevenoaks taken at the same spot as the previous photograph. *LGRP 16628*

157
A down express near Chelsfield hauled by 'D' class No 75. *LGRP 16617*

158
The pioneer 'K' class 2-6-4T No 790 passing Chelsfield in August 1923 with a down passenger train for Ashford. *LGRP 16633*

159
A suburban passenger train approaching Purley about 1923 headed by 'J' class 0-6-4T No 597. *LGRP 20201*

159

South Eastern & Chatham Locomotives

Harry S. Wainwright took over as Locomotive, Carriage & Wagon Superintendent on 1 January 1899 when the working union of the LCDR and the SER came into force, the stock of both companies being his responsibility. On that date the SER possessed 459 locomotives and the LCDR 215 and to avoid confusion it was decided to renumber the LCDR locomotives by adding 459 to their existing numbers.

Many old locomotives still in service were in urgent need of replacement so as an interim measure before new locomotives could be designed five 4-4-0 tender engines were purchased from Neilson, Reid and 15 0-4-4 side tanks based on the LCDR 'R' class were ordered from Sharp, Stewart.

The 4-4-0s were designed by William Pickersgill of the Great North of Scotland Railway and formed part of an order of 10 engines by that company which were no longer required as a result of the GNSR's financial difficulties. They were numbered 676-680 on the SECR and classified 'G' and although they were at first put to work on the principal expresses their indifferent performance meant they were soon relegated to slower trains. Nos 676 and 679 were rebuilt in 1914 with boilers purchased secondhand from the GNR and they were all withdrawn between 1924 and 1927.

The 0-4-4Ts were numbered 696-710 and were known as the 'R1' class and all entered service in late 1900 joining the earlier 'R' class on the London suburban trains. All except two were later rebuilt with 'H' class boilers, these two (withdrawn in 1929) being the only ones not to be taken over by British Railways in 1948. After Grouping electrification in the London area meant that most of them were transferred away from London but other duties were found for them and it was not until 1956 that the last one was withdrawn.

Wainwright's first design, the 'C' class 0-6-0 goods, entered service in 1900 and proved so successful that a total of 109 engines had been built when construction ceased in 1908. Only nine were built at Longhedge, these engines, built

between 1902 and 1904, being the last built there. They were the principal main line goods locomotives until just before Grouping when they began to be replaced by the 'N' class 2-6-0s. The first withdrawal was in 1947 but all the remainder of the class entered BR stock the following year. Withdrawal did not start in earnest until the late 1950s and it was 1967 before the last engine was withdrawn.

Wainwright's first express passenger locomotives were the 'D' class 4-4-0s introduced in 1901. They were handsome engines with 6ft 8in coupled wheels, 51 being built between 1901 and 1908. Following successful rebuilding of 11 of the later 'E' class 4-4-0s in 1919/20, it was decided to treat the 'Ds' in a similar manner so between 1921 and 1927 21 'Ds' were rebuilt as 'D1s', the first 10 by Beyer, Peacock and the remainder by Ashford Works. The 'Ds' worked the principal expresses until they were displaced in the mid-1920s when they were relegated to slower services but only two were withdrawn before 1948 and the last six survived until 1956. Those engines rebuilt as 'D1s' at first worked the heaviest expresses but they were eventually displaced by 'King Arthurs' in the early 1930s. One engine was withdrawn before Nationalisation, as a result of war damage in 1944, but the last 17 survived until between 1959 and 1961.

The first of Wainwright's well known 'H' class 0-4-4Ts was built in 1904, the first of a class of 66 engines, all of which were built at Ashford between 1904 and 1915. As would be expected after the success of the Kirtley 'R' class and the later 'R1s', these engines formed the basis for the new design but larger cylinders and slightly larger boilers were used. They mostly worked suburban trains in the London area, especially on the South Eastern lines where they were a great improvement on the Stirling 'Qs' but after Grouping they were more scattered. The first two withdrawals were made in 1944 but seven years elapsed before the next one and 33 were still in service at the end of 1960, the last three all being withdrawn in January 1964.

Two secondhand engines were acquired in

1904. No 751 was purchased from the LBSCR for working the Isle of Sheppey Light Railway being one of that company's famous 'Terriers'. Like many of that class, it had a long life having been built in 1876 and not withdrawn until 1962. The other engine was a Manning Wardle 0-6-0ST, No 752, which was purchased from a William Rigby who was a contractor working at Folkestone Harbour.

Two steam railcars entered service in 1905, the four-coupled engine units being built by Kitson and the carriage units, which had 56 seats of one class, being built by the Metropolitan Railway Carriage & Wagon Company. They were purchased in an attempt to cut operating costs on branch lines and, after a series of successful trials, six further railcars were purchased, these entering service in 1906. They were not a success in service, however, proving unpopular with both footplate men and passengers. Their riding was rough and when they were required to pull a fully laden trailer they lacked sufficient power to keep time. All eight were officially withdrawn in April 1924 but none of them had worked for four years and one of them hadn't worked for nearly 10 years.

Another class of 4-4-0 express passenger engine, the 'E' class, was introduced in 1906. They were generally similar to the 'Ds' but they had larger fireboxes of the Belpaire type which necessitated a longer wheelbase. A total of 26 were built, all at Ashford and the last in 1909, and they joined the 'Ds' in working the principal expresses. Two engines, Nos 36 and 275, were rebuilt with superheaters in 1912 but, although they were an immediate success, their increased axle loading prevented their use on the LCDR section and no more were similarly rebuilt. In 1919 No 179 was rebuilt at Ashford in an attempt to produce a more powerful engine with an axle load which did not exceed $17\frac{1}{2}$ tons. This was done by increasing the grate area, adding a superheater and fitting new cylinders with long travel piston valves and making many alterations which included the cab, splashers and running plate to reduce the weight. In 1920 a further 10 engines were similarly rebuilt by Beyer, Peacock, the rebuilds being reclassified 'E1'. The first 'E1s' to be withdrawn went between 1949 and 1951 before any of the original 'Es' but although the last 'E' was withdrawn in 1955 the seven remaining 'E1s' lasted longer, being withdrawn between 1958 and 1961.

In an attempt to resolve the difficulties experienced with the steam railcars two small 0-6-0Ts were built in 1909 and, after trials with them proved successful, a further six were built the following year. They were put to work on light passenger trains but, although they were more successful than the railcars, when it became necessary to increase their load to four coaches this proved too much for them. They were eventually displaced by larger tank engines and later they worked at Dover and Folkestone but all eight were still in service at nationalisation and the last withdrawal was not made until 1961.

In 1913 a class of five large 0-6-4Ts was built at Ashford. The smaller 0-4-4Ts then in widespread use had barely sufficient coal and water capacity for the longer trips, the new engines, known as Class J, being built to rectify this. They had 5ft 6in coupled wheels and superheated Belpaire boilers but they were indifferent performers so an order for five more was cancelled. They were withdrawn between 1949 and 1951.

The weight restrictions on the LCDR section had long prevented the introduction of larger locomotives but by 1913 the need had become urgent enough for the decision to be made to build a class of large 4-4-0s for the South Eastern section only. The result was the 'L' class of 22 engines all of which were built in 1914, Nos 760-771 by Beyer, Peacock and Nos 772-781 by A. Borsig of Berlin, the latter arriving only a few weeks before the outbreak of war. They had 6ft 6in coupled wheels and superheated Belpaire boilers of 5ft 0in diameter and they quickly proved successful on the best South Eastern section expresses. After Grouping they were displaced by 'King Arthurs' and 'Schools' but, nevertheless, they all entered BR stock in 1948, the final withdrawals being made in 1961.

Soon after the formation of the Managing Committee it was decided to concentrate the carriage and wagon work at Ashford. The existing shops there were to be extended and work and machinery transferred there from Longhedge which was to be gradually run down. It was later decided to close Longhedge and transfer all its remaining work to Ashford but, as part of the Board's policy of rationalisation and cost reduction, Longhedge was closed before there was sufficient capacity at Ashford to handle all the work. This resulted in serious delays in the repair of locomotives and consequent motive power shortages, much of the blame for this falling unfairly on Wainwright who became the scapegoat for bad decisions by the Board. The outcome was that Wainwright was retired on 30 November 1913, although he was only 48, and replaced by Richard Maunsell who, with a new team of assistants recruited from other companies, set about designing a series of locomotive classes capable of handling all the company's trains. It was eventually agreed to order 10 2-6-0 tender engines and six 2-6-4T engines from Ashford Works but work on them was delayed by the war and it was 1917 before one engine of each type was completed. The 2-6-4T, No 790 known as Class K, was the only one of its class to be built before Grouping but the Southern Railway built 19 more in 1925/26 and named them after rivers. After the Sevenoaks accident on 24 August 1927 when No A800 *River Cray* left the rails at speed, they were all withdrawn from service and converted to 2-6-0 tender engines. They were reclassified 'U' and 30 similar engines were built between 1928 and 1931.

The 2-6-0 No 810, known as Class N, had 5ft 6in coupled wheels, 6in smaller than No 790's, and a superheated domeless taper boiler of the same type as that fitted to the 2-6-4T. It was built as a heavy goods engine and was a great improvement on existing engines. From 1920 to 1923 14 more were built followed in 1924/25 by a further 50 built from parts supplied by Woolwich Arsenal and another 15 built from 1932 to 1934.

The SECR handed over 729 engines to the newly formed Southern Railway on 1 January 1923. Maunsell was appointed Chief Mechanical Engineer and many other SECR men were appointed to senior positions in the locomotive department which meant that SECR practice influenced the locomotives built by the Southern for many years. Shortly after the formation of the Southern Railway a three-cylinder version of the 'N' class, 'N1' No 822, with Holcroft's derived valve gear for the inside cylinder, was completed

at Ashford and in 1925 followed a three-cylinder 2-6-4T version, 'K1' No 890. Other classes which had a direct link with earlier SECR classes were the 15 'L1' class 4-4-0s built in 1926, the 15 'W' class 2-6-4Ts built between 1931 and 1936 and the 20 'U1' class 2-6-0s built in 1931.

160
'G' class 4-4-0 No 677, one of the engines diverted from an order by the Great North of Scotland Railway. *LPC 33051*

161
'C' class 0-6-0 No 54 which was built at Ashford in 1901 and withdrawn in 1960 as BR No 31054. *LGRP 8139*

162
'R1' class 0-4-4T No 708, one of a class of 15 engines, all of which were built by Sharp, Stewart & Co in 1900. *LPC 15570*

160

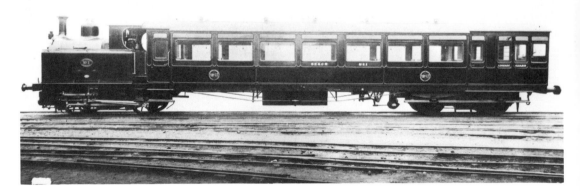

163
'D' class 4-4-0 No 246 which was built at Ashford in 1902 and rebuilt to Class D1 in 1921. *LPC 33082*

164
Steam railcar No 1, the first of its type, which was delivered to the SECR on 16 January 1905.
LPC 33054

165
'P' class 0-6-0T No 325 standing in Greenwich Park station in July 1912 after conversion for push and pull working. *LPC 33158*

166
In 1917 'C' class 0-6-0 No 685 was converted to a saddle tank for shunting at Richborough and reclassified 'S'. It was transferred to Bricklayers Arms in 1919 and was withdrawn in 1951 as No 1685.
LPC 33098

166

167
'J' class 0-6-4T No 129 at Bricklayers Arms in May 1920. It was renumbered A596 by the Southern and was withdrawn in 1951 as BR No 31596, the last survivor of the class. *LGRP 14598*

168
'N' class 2-6-0 No 810 at Bricklayers Arms in May 1920. *LGRP 14602*

169
0-6-0T No 751 at Ashford in May 1920. This engine was built in 1876 at Brighton Works and was originally LBSCR No 54 *Waddon*, its number being altered to 654 in January 1900. It was withdrawn in 1904 and purchased by the SECR who renumbered it 751 which it retained until December 1932 when the Southern transferred it to Service Stock as No 680s. It finally became DS680 in May 1952 and was withdrawn in 1962, eventually being preserved in Canada.
RP W5972

170
0-6-0ST No 752, a Manning Wardle engine which was built in 1879 for a contractor called Joseph Firbank who gave it the name *Grinstead*. In 1899 it was sold to William Rigby, a contractor working at Folkestone Harbour, and renamed *Middleton* and he sold it to the SECR in 1904. *RP W5958*

168

171
'L' class 4-4-0 No 767 in wartime austerity livery.
LPC 15472

172
'H' class 0-4-4T No 540. *LPC 33176*

173
'C' class 0-6-0 No 498 photographed at Battersea.
LPC 33044

174
'D' class 4-4-0 No 488 at Battersea in September
1921. *LGRP 14623*

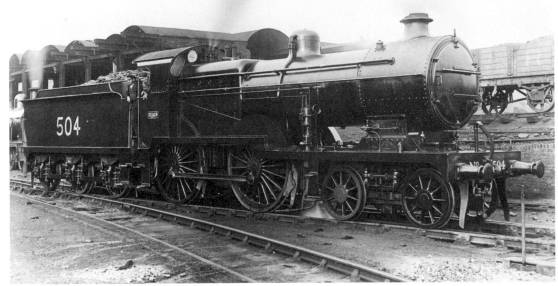

175
'E1' class 4-4-0 No 504 at Battersea in September
1921 after being rebuilt from Class E by Beyer, Peacock
& Co in April 1920. *LGRP 14618*

176
'E' class 4-4-0 No 273 at Battersea in September 1921
as fitted with extended smokebox and cast chimney
with capuchon. *LGRP 14624*

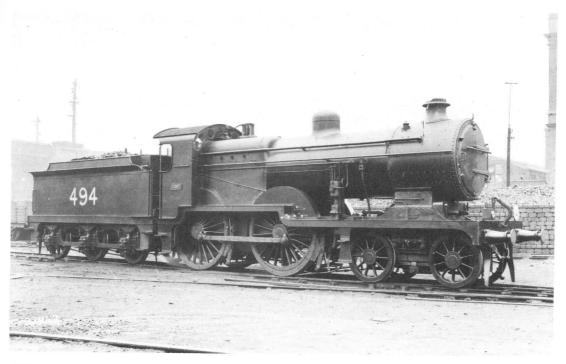

177
'D1' class 4-4-0 No 494 after being rebuilt from
Class D by Beyer, Peacock & Co in August 1921.
LPC 33042

178
'E' class 4-4-0 No 515 at Bricklayers Arms in June
1924 as fitted with extended smokebox and cast
chimney without capuchon.   *LGRP 14662*

179
'N' class 2-6-0 No 823 at Bricklayers Arms in June 1924. This engine was the first of the class to enter service after Grouping (in May 1923). *LGRP 14659*

180
The pioneer 'K' class 2-6-4T as SR No A790 after being named *River Avon* in January 1925. It was rebuilt as a 'U' class 2-6-0 in 1928. *LPC 33195*

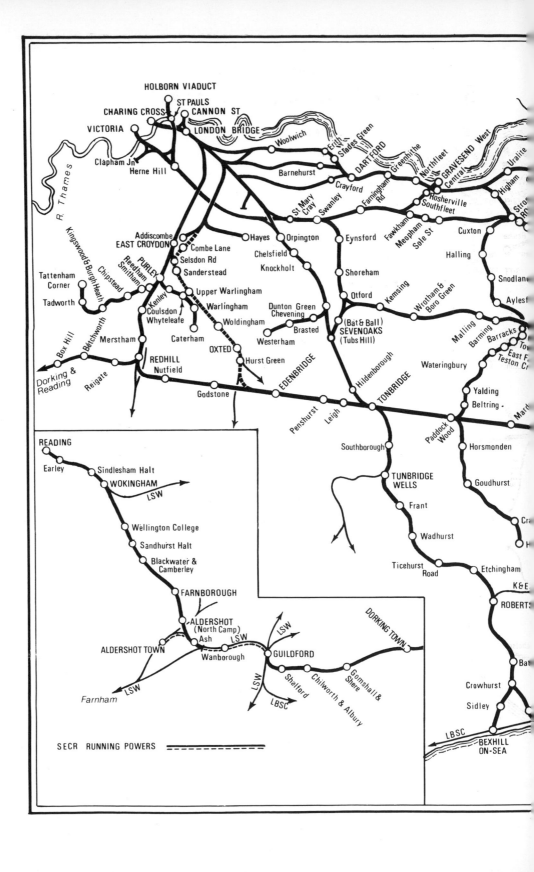